SUPERMARKET
TRICKS

SUPERMARKET TRICKS

More Than 125 Ways to Improvise Good Sex

by Jay Wiseman

Published in the United States by Greenery Press, 3739 Balboa Ave. #195, San Francisco, CA 94121.

http://www.bigrock.com/~greenery
verdant@crl.com

ISBN #0-9639763-4-6

Table of Contents

Acknowledgments
(The Thank You List)

All the people below contributed Tricks, or other useful information, to this book. My heartfelt thanks to all.

Bob Shurtleff	KJ
Cecilia Tan	Lana White
Belladonna	Libby Donahue
Chilo	Lynn Craig
China	Maggi Rubenstein
Derek	Mic Bergen
Elf Sternberg	Nightlace
Francesca Guido	Snow White
Hal	Teresa
Irish	Tom Burns
Jaymes Easton	Wakinyan Cikala
John Warren	Wilhelmina Moosepunch
Kim Airs	

Finally, major thanks, and all my love, to Janet – who once again has proven indispensable in the creation of this book. I love you absolutely, unconditionally, and with all my heart, just the way you are.

Warning and Disclaimer

There is no such thing as risk-free sex, especially these days. Sexual behavior, and the personal, interpersonal, and broader implications of what it means, can be intense, powerful matters.

In the medical world, there's a dictum about administering medication that involves the "five rights": Give the right drug to the right patient in the right way with the right dosage at the right time. A similar outlook can apply to sexuality. Being sexual with the right person, in the right way, at the right time, in the right location, and for the right reasons can be an incredibly positive experience for everyone involved. In any of the above is not right, however, then problems, sometimes very severe – even life-destroying – problems can emerge.

Erotic energy is one of the most powerful forces in our world. Respect and pay attention to that power and you can experience bliss. Disrespect or ignore that power and you might not live to regret it.

The primary purpose of "Supermarket Tricks" is to provide information and advice that will help make good sex between informed, consenting adults a little bit better. It also provides basic information to help people understand their situations, make them aware of possible alternatives, cope with problems, and find helpful resources.

Please do not think of this book as any kind of medical, legal, psychological, or other professional advice. It most certainly is not intended as a substitute for proper sex therapy. Most of its core information, particularly the "Tricks" themselves, was discovered on my own, taught to me by lovers I have had, shared with me by friends during highly informal conversations (many has been the time since the first "Tricks" book was published that someone has come up to me and said "I've got a Trick for you"), or sent to me either in the mail or over the Internet. Please keep that in mind when considering this book's contents.

Almost without question, there are at least a few factual errors in this book, and probably a few typographical errors as well. Also, it's very common, in this and many other fields, that information believed to be accurate at the time of publication is later revealed to be inaccurate – sometimes only slightly so, sometimes very much so. If you have even the slightest question about the accuracy or safety of anything in here, please check with independent sources. If their recommendations differ from mine, please let me know. By the way, please remember that not all professional advice is equally complete, accurate, up-to-date, and unbiased. By all means get an independent "second opinion" (and maybe even a "third opinion") if you feel even the slightest need for it.

If you think you have found a factual error, typographical error, or other inaccuracy or omission in this book, please let me know so that this can be corrected in future printings.

No one associated with writing, editing, printing, distributing, or selling this book, or in any other way associated with it, is in any way liable for any damages that result from acting on the information herein. While I have most certainly not put anything in here that I consider likely to be harmful, understand clearly that you act on the information in this book entirely at your own risk.

How Did "Supermarket Tricks" Come To Be?

Sex and Creativity

For many years now, the study of creative thinking has been a moderately serious hobby of mine. Many people feel there is something frivolous, redundant, or unnecessary about such study. After all, being creative seems all-too-obvious to them, and the idea the it could be studied or taught is ridiculous.

That has not been my experience. Indeed, I have found that the ability to think creatively definitely needs to be cultivated, nourished, and even protected – very much like a garden. As a writer, I sometimes think of myself as an "idea farmer." I plant the seed of an idea, help it to grow and be fruitful and, finally, pay the rent with it by selling the fruits of my idea and my labor (my book) on the marketplace.

Sadly, and all too often, any sign of creativity or innovative thinking is vigorously suppressed. Even among relatively enlightened people, the impulse to preserve the status quo is strong and almost reflexive. As the noted creative thinking expert Edward De Bono once wrote, "Most people look at a new idea just long enough to find a reason to reject it." Because the ability to think creatively is a major job skill of mine, I've found that more and more I limit how much time I spend around people who are highly negative in their outlook and judgments. If I had listened to them, I probably would have written very little by now, and published even less.

Creativity is very important in our daily lives. If I, as a writer, don't come up with anything new and valuable to communicate, I'm out

3

of a job. Sometimes our very survival depends on our creativity. During my days as an ambulance crewman, sometimes the patient's survival (and, occasionally, my own) depended on my ability to find a new way to cope with an emergency situation. Indeed, it's been speculated that our very survival as a species on this planet depends on our ability to come up with creative new approaches to the problems facing us.

Creativity is not at all something lightweight or frivolous. It can be a valuable job skill. It can even be a form of survival training.

One of the creativity principles that I learned by reading De Bono's books was that you can often get a greater net gain in a situation by improving something that's already working well than you can by solving a problem associated with that situation (although, of course, you should work on the problems, too).

Back in 1992, I decided to take that way of looking at things and apply it to sex. It only took me a moment to realize that virtually every lover of mine had something she did to improve our sex life just slightly. It might have been a special way that she used her hand or her mouth, or a particular way she arranged things, or how she smoothed out something that would otherwise have been awkward. I also saw that, over the years, I had thought of several on my own. I named these behaviors "Tricks" and decided to write a book about them.

Thus, in October of 1992, the book was born. I named it "Tricks!: More Than 125 Ways to Make Good Sex Better." It was a delightful little book – fun to write (and to research!), easy to market, and just generally pleasant all the way around. What I didn't suspect at the time was that I had created something of an ever-so-gentle monster – a monster that gradually began to take on a life of its own.

My friends started coming up to me and saying "I've got a Trick for you." Occasionally, during our own lovemaking, Janet or I would say "hey, that's a Trick." (I keep a notepad by our bed.) People sent me Tricks in the mail. Eventually, the situation reached "critical mass" and in

February of 1994 "Tricks 2: Another 125 Ways to Make Good Sex Better" came out.

In May of 1994, after I got on the Internet (I'm jaybob@crl.com) I starting getting "Tricks from cyberspace." The procession of Tricks just, as it were, kept on coming.

I realized that I had a "logical gap" in my line of books. I had my "Tricks" books to give people tips regarding how to use their bodies and items found in the average household, and I had "SM 101: A Realistic Introduction" to tell people how to get started in SM play, and to use things like whips, clamps, leather cuffs, and so forth, but I didn't have anything on how to use sex toys that weren't SM toys, such as dildoes, vibrators, and so forth. Thus was born the idea for "Sex Toy Tricks: More Than 125 Ways To Accessorize Good Sex." After some exhaustive research (!) and a long series of consultations, the book itself came out in April of 1995.

(I have since had ample opportunity to contemplate the fact that, for the rest of my life, I'm now the author of "SM 101" and "Sex Toy Tricks." Talk about your highly specialized resumes!)

While contemplating what should be in "Sex Toy Tricks" the following idea floated through my head: Say, you've got some Tricks on how to use household items in both your "Tricks" and "Tricks 2" books, and you make reference to them in your "Sex Toy Tricks" book. How about an *entire book* just on using household items? The idea was an immediate hit and, of course, once again "the game was afoot." Yeah, I know, I've got a *really* tough job!

So now, after even more months of demanding research, brainstorming, and conferring, I humbly present you with my latest offering. I very much hope you enjoy "Supermarket Tricks." I'd be very happy to hear your comments regarding it; of course, look for "Supermarket Tricks 2" sometime in the future.

Happy shopping!

Jay Wiseman
San Francisco, CA

Assumptions

In presenting the material in this book, I am making the following assumptions about your situation. If any of these assumptions are not true in your case, please modify your behavior accordingly.

I'm assuming:

1. That both of you are willing (and, hopefully, eager) to have sex with each other. Consent is absolutely essential.

2. That being sexual with each other will not violate any agreements you have made with others about your sexual behavior.

3. That both of you reasonably understand what you are doing. Having sex with someone too young, senile, feeble-minded, intoxicated, or otherwise unable to fully understand and consent to what is happening may get you charged with rape, even if no force was used. (Having sex with an unconscious person can also get you charged with rape.) If they're too drunk to drive, they're probably too drunk to have sex.

4. That both of you have reached the age of consent in your state (and that you live in the United States). I believe the age of consent is as low as 12 in a few states and as high as 18 in many others. An act that is perfectly legal on one side of a state line may get you a lengthy prison sentence if done on the other side of it. Make sure you know the age of consent in your state.

Your local library should have a copy of your state's criminal code in its reference section. Reading its sections on rape, incest, indecent exposure, lewd and lascivious behavior, assault, contribution to the deliquency of a minor, and related sections may be very instructive. Asking a local attorney or police officer (who you already know well) can also help, but remember that opinions, knowledge, and objectivity can vary widely, even among such "experts." Try to get information from more than one source.

(By the way, sex between blood relatives may be illegal no matter what the age of those involved. If you cannot legally marry a particular person, it may also be illegal for you to have sex with each other. This could be true even if both of you are over 18 and both fully consent.)

5. That the acts I'm describing are legal in your state. Although the laws are rarely enforced, oral sex, anal intercourse, and other practices are still a crime in some states, even if done by consenting adults in private. (Possession of some sorts of sex toys is against the law in some areas.) Find out your state's laws and, where appropriate, work to change them. This whole area is badly in need of legislative reform.

6. That no risk exists of passing on a sexually transmitted disease. These days, that's a *big* assumption. If such a risk does exist, please modify what you do. Among other things, if you have herpes or have tested positive for the HIV virus and have sex with someone without first telling them about that, you could be arrested. If your partner becomes infected, you could also be sued. If you have any questions, one source of information is the National Sexually Transmitted Disease Hotline at (800) 227-8922.

Criteria

For inclusion in this book, a Trick usually had to meet the following criteria:

1. It had to be something that could be done pretty much on impulse in the here and now. Nothing too elaborate.

2. It had to involve items found around the average household, or easily purchased in a store found in the average neighborhood – a supermarket, hardware store, stationery store or similar establishment.

3. It had to be safe. I included nothing I thought likely to endanger people.

4. It had to pertain directly to sex or to a very closely related matter.

5. It had to have a successful track record. I looked for Tricks that had consistently made more than one lover gasp, sigh, and moan.

6. It had to appeal to a wide, mainstream audience. The Trick couldn't be too far out or kinky. (Again, that's another book.) Most of the Tricks therefore involve masturbation, fellatio, cunnilingus, vaginal penetration, and anal penetration.

Selection, Balance, and Orientation

The Tricks in this book are largely a reflection of the material I received. I interviewed dozens of Tricksters, male and female, gay, straight, and bisexual, to come up with the Tricks you see here.

I've tried to present as many Tricks as possible in a "gender neutral" manner. In most cases, it doesn't matter whether the people involved are straight, bisexual or gay.

Please remember that I publish a series of "Tricks" books. If you feel a certain category is under-represented, by all means send in material to balance things out.

I deliberately included many masturbation Tricks in this book as my own way of encouraging safer sex.

I decided to, for the most part, leave out material regarding SM, swinging, tantra, multiple-partner sex, and so forth. Those are specialized areas, and their practices and customs are far too extensive to describe properly in this book. I included contact information regarding them if you're interested in exploring them further. You may also find useful information in some of my other books (listed on the last page).

The Limits Of Tricks

You know, and I know, that lovemaking cannot and should not be reduced to Tricks. Tricks are to erotic play what spices are to eating. A few carefully chosen ones make the experience more intense and pleasurable. Too many spoil things.

It's entirely possible to have a wonderful and completely satisfying sex life without knowing the Tricks in this book, or any others. Good sex is based on caring about your partner's well-being, really wanting to have sex with them (and, of course them really wanting to have sex with you), and observing the responsibilities that go along with that. Still, adding a carefully chosen spice now and then helps things along.

Key Point: Your underlying feelings towards the other person, and theirs toward you, greatly affect whether or not a Trick will improve your erotic play. As one lady told me, "If I really like him, then he almost can't do anything wrong. If I really don't like him, then he can't even breathe right."

When a Trick Bombs

Each person has their own unique physical and emotional pattern of erotic responsiveness. Every now and then a Trick that has always worked well before may utterly turn off this particular partner. The key phrase for handling this situation is "show compassion for everyone, including yourself."

If what you did *really* turned your partner off, try not to take it personally. (You wouldn't be human if you didn't take it somewhat personally, but don't buy into that too deeply.) Remember, each person has their own pattern, and you can never completely know what that pattern looks like. Give them a brief apology, if that seems appropriate, then move on to something else. There is little to be gained by debating the point, particularly right then. Save discussions for later.

On the other hand, if your partner starts to do something that really doesn't work for you, diplomatically let them know that as soon as you can. Being "polite" in this situation will only allow your displeasure to build to uncontrollable levels. Speak up (politely, please) as soon as possible. Remember, this is almost undoubtedly not willful misconduct on their part. They are probably doing it in an attempt, however misguided, to turn you on. Speak up, but give them the benefit of the doubt, especially if this partner is relatively new.

Find Their Envelope

Each person has their own erotic response pattern, something I've come to think of as their "envelope." One of your main tasks as a good lover is to find your partner's envelope. The envelope varies considerably. Something that is wildly erotic for one person can be grossly unpleasant, and even traumatic, for another.

The envelope varies widely from person to person. It also varies over time with the same person. Find their envelope before you try too many Tricks, and remember that the location and content of that envelope change over time.

Sex and the Internet

In the last few years, the international computer network known as the Internet has skyrocketed in usage – particularly its sexuality-related areas.

Some places on the Internet, devoted to the discussion of specific subjects, are called newsgroups. There, people can read and place messages related to the topic. Several thousand newsgroups exist and about 100 new ones appear each month. In addition, thousands of pages on the World Wide Web are devoted to sexuality issues – search engines such as Yahoo can help you find them. If you're interested in aviation, bicycling, stamp collecting, MTV, or virtually any other subject, you can find an international network of kindred spirits on the net.

More than a dozen newsgroups are devoted to various aspects of sexuality. Most are called "alt" (for alternative) groups. Some of the best-known are:

alt.sex   alt.sex.masturbation

alt.sex.bondage   alt.polyamory

alt.sex.swingers   alt.sexual.abuse.recovery

alt.sex.anal   alt.transgendered

alt.sex.enemas   alt.politics.sex

alt.sex.safe   alt.recovery.sexual.addiction

alt.sex.stories   alt.sex.wizards

In addition, two newsgroups exist for the sole purpose of marketing sex-related goods. Check out alt.sex.marketplace and alt.sex.erotica.marketplace (the busier of the two) for more information. I can be reached as jaybob@crl.com on the 'Net.

The Neurology of Tricks

To help understand how Tricks work, it can be useful to understand a bit about how the human nervous system is organized. The following highly simplified summary may help.

The nervous system is composed of two primary parts: the central nervous system and the peripheral nervous system. The central nervous system consists of the brain and spinal cord. The peripheral nervous system consists of sensory nerves, motor nerves, and the nerves of the autonomic nervous system. (The autonomic nerves handle the "fight or flight" actions of what's called the sympathetic nervous system and the "feed and breed" actions of what's called the parasympathetic nervous system.)

The nervous system is mostly concerned with impulses flowing to and from the brain. As Tricksters, we are mainly concerned with impulses that flow to the brain. These impulses originate in the various sensory organs – eyes, ears, skin, etc. – and from fibers that sense both body position (known as proprioception) and degree of muscle stretch.

There are several different "bundles" of neurons (nerve cells) in the spinal cord, called tracts. There are both descending tracts (that carry info down from the brain), and ascending tracts (that carry info up to the brain). We're primarily concerned with ascending tracts.

Regarding the sense of touch, the human body can sense five basic types: light touch, heavy touch, warmth, cold, and pain. The sense of heavy touch is further broken down by some authorities into pressure, crude touch, and vibration.

The sensory nerves that branch off the spinal column (and those that come directly off the brain, called the cranial nerves) each serve a different part of the body. Imagine a human body sitting on the ground with its arms and legs sticking straight out to the side. Each nerve has a given lateral "segment" of the body that it covers. Consult a medical book for a "dermatome map" and you'll see what I mean. In each dermatome, there's a sensory nerve that carries input back to the spinal cord.

Different ascending tracts in the spinal cord carry different types of information back up to the brain. Warmth, cold, and pain are handled by the lateral spinothalmic tract. Muscle stretch and position sense are handled by both the anterior and posterior spino-cerebellar tracts. Crude touch and pressure and handled by the anterior spinothalmic tract. Light touch and vibration are handled by the posterior or dorsal columns.

This information gives us clues as to why Tricks can make erotic play more intense. Many of them involve combining different types of stimulation in the same area, thus allowing a more intense sensory input per unit area of skin. For example, if you apply pressure, vibration, and warmth all at the same time to a given area of skin, such as the skin covering the genitals, you get a huge increase in the total amount of sensory information being sent to the brain from that area.

A Note About "Numbing Out" and Pain

Many people report that the amount of sensation they feel when a vibrator, for example, is applied to them drops off after a while – in some cases, quite rapidly. The neurological term for this is "adaptation." Put simply, we don't need to be aware of all the input we're receiving all the time. It's better if we can concentrate or focus our attention and awareness. That being so, the nervous system filters out what it regards as low-priority information. Touch is often deemed low-priority information, particularly light touch (until I mention it, you're probably not aware of the sock covering your left foot) but also for pressure and vibration. Thus your brain may begin to "screen it out" after it no longer seems like "new information" and you'll feel that sensation less as time passes.

A Possible Neurological Clue to the Appeal of SM

The brain usually adapts very rapidly to light touch, pressure, and vibration, but adapts very slowly to body position – and adapts hardly at all to pain. Thus Tricks that involve a new body position may be more "interesting" to the brain than Tricks involving light touch. We thus have at least a partial clue as to why some people find SM play intriguing. Pain is the strongest, most constant, sensation the body can experience. If this sensation can be eroticized, and if the experience that accompanied receiving it could be made not too damaging to the body, the erotic potential, for *some* people, could be nothing short of extraordinary.

A Few Don'ts Regarding Tricks

1. Don't spend too much time doing Tricks. It's far more important to stay in the here and now with your lover. Do a Trick "every now and then."

2. Don't do too many different Tricks in a single session. Again, that distances you from your lover.

3. Don't look too hard for opportunities to do a Trick. Let such opportunities appear naturally. Men seem particularly vulnerable to this pitfall, giving rise to the somewhat bitter saying among women, "There were three of us in bed: him, me, and his technique."

4. Never place anything in a woman's vagina if it's recently been in her (or anyone else's) anus. Doing so can cause an infection that will require a doctor's visit and antibiotics to cure. (A physician once told me that licking a woman's anus and then licking her vulva could cause her to get infected.) Anything used for anal play must be thoroughly cleaned before being used for vaginal play.

5. Never seal your mouth over a woman's vagina and blow into it. Women have suffered fatal air embolisms from this practice. Menstruating women and pregnant women face higher than average risk. Such incidents are rare, but they do happen.

6. Be careful about placing food items, especially sugary foods, in a woman's vagina. Many men and women recommended placing foods in there and then eating them out (grapes had something of a cult following). These foods can upset the vagina's natural pH balance and cause infections, particularly yeast infections. One of my Tricksters recommends placing a Reality female condom in her vagina, then filling *that* with food, if you want to play this way.

Intoxicants

Provided you don't have a substance abuse problem, light use of intoxicants can do a lot to enhance your mood. They can relax tense muscles, take your mind off the worries of the day, and calm you down and bring you into the here and now.

I prefer wine. Beer tends to fill up my bladder too quickly (and too often). Harder liquors take me more out of it than I like. I quit using recreational drugs of any kind many years ago.

More than light intoxicant use is asking for trouble. Your judgment becomes dangerously cloudy. Your coordination suffers. You may become too out of it to be sexual at all.

AIDS prevention experts are campaigning against combining sex and intoxicants. They have found that many unsafe sex acts occur when, and – more importantly – only when the people involved are intoxicated. They compare driving under the influence (D.U.I.) with having sex under the influence (S.U.I.) in terms of danger.

Remember that getting someone too drunk or stoned to understand what is happening and then having sex with them is rape.

As a rule, if you get someone too drunk or stoned that it would be a crime for them to drive, then it would also probably be a crime to have sex with them.

About the Handcuff Icon

When you see this icon appearing next to a Trick anywhere in this book, that means that particular Trick may involve significant amounts of strong sensation, helplessness or other SM-like experiences. Before you try any of these Tricks, *please* read the section entitled "Safety Tips for S/M and Erotic Power Play" starting on Page 75.

SUPERMARKET TRICKS

Let's start at the very beginning.

This is a book about how to use items that someone could buy in an ordinary store to improve their sex life. That being so, it seems obvious to point out that the average, well-equipped drug store or supermarket contains a number of items specifically intended to be used during sex. So, before we rush off to the more exotic locales, let's drop by the pharmacy section and see what they have there.

Here are 12 items that can be found in a well-stocked drugstore and are specifically intended to be used before, during, or after sex.

● ● ● ● ●

1

● ● ● ●

Lubricants

There are various oil-based and water-based lubricants on the market specifically intended to make sexual intercourse easier. These come both with and without nonoxynol-9. Because oil dissolves latex, only water-based lubricants should be used with a latex condom. Take a few minutes and look over the lubricant selection. Note which brands are water-based and which are oil-based. Note which brands contain nonoxynol-9 and which don't.

● ● ● ● ● ●

2.
Latex Condoms

These are perhaps the most well-known item sold in an
average supermarket or pharmacy for use during sex.
Latex condoms come in different sizes and a wide
variety of types. Some are ribbed; some are
not. Some are lubricated; some are not.

3.
Polyurethane Condoms

More and more people are discovering that they are
at least somewhat allergic to latex. Fortunately,
a new, ultra-thin polyurethane condom named the
"Avanti" is now on the market. This condom can be used
with oil-based lubricants; however, there have been
reports of higher-than-usual breakage rates, so be careful.
(One occasionally sees lambskin condoms on the market.
These condoms "leak" virus in a way that latex and
polyurethane do not, so their usage is falling out of favor.)

4.
Female Condoms

A condom for the woman to wear inside her vagina is
called the "Reality" condom and is a polyurethane type. A
small packet of lubricant is included.

5.

Contraceptive Foams, Films and Gels

Most of these contain nonoxynol-9 and are inserted before intercourse. Some brands can be used alone, others should be used in connection with a condom or diaphragm. Some need a special applicator (that comes with the product) and some do not. See the package instructions for details.

6.

Spermicidal Suppositories

Like most foams, films, and gels, these also contain nonoxynol-9. They are highly portable and easy to use. One caution is that they may be wax-based, and so perhaps not the best type to use with a condom. On the other hand, a spermicidal suppository or two can be inserted "after the fact" if the condom breaks or falls off and may help provide some protection. More on this later.

7.

Nonoxynol-9 Alternative

If you're sensitive to nonoxynol-9, consider trying its "cousin" octoxynol-9. Look for the Ortho-Gynol brand.

.8.
Basal Metabolic Thermometers

These are thermometers which measure temperature more precisely than regular thermometers measure it – i.e., in tenths of a degree. They are used by some women to detect the subtle changes in body temperature that accompany ovulation.

.9.
Lubricating Suppositories

These suppositories are usually made of glycerin or some other condom-compatible substance. They provide additional vaginal lubrication that's often useful to older women.

.10.
Numbing Creams

Creams containing a local anesthetic are available. These are intended for men to apply to their penis shortly before intercourse to help them from reaching orgasm too quickly. The most popular brand for this is called Detane. Whether or not this cream is safe for use with condoms is not known. Men who suffer from chronic or severe problems regarding premature ejaculation should consult their physician or a sex therapist.

.11.

Pregnancy Test Kits

It is now possible to by inexpensive, highly reliable kits that you can use privately to test for pregnancy. Be sure to read the directions carefully and follow them exactly.

.12.

Ovulation Test Kits

Recently home ovulation test kits have appeared on the marketplace. These can be used to help time intercourse to either help promote or prevent pregnancy.

"Supplemental" sexual items. The following items, while not specifically intended to be used during sex, can certainly have relevance.

.13.

Latex Gloves

These come in a variety of colors and sizes and are relatively inexpensive. Powder-free gloves are also available if you're sensitive to talcum.

14
Vinyl Gloves

These are perhaps not quite as close-fitting as latex gloves, but they certainly work well enough for almost all uses. They're a useful option for people who are allergic to latex.

15
Nail Files and Emery Boards

If you enjoy sticking your fingers into various parts of your partner's body, a careful smoothing of your nails beforehand will be most welcome. Running your nails along the underside of your opposite forearm is a time-honored testing method of determining whether or not they're smooth enough.

16
DiamonDeb Nail File

This is a special type of nail file, coated with diamond dust, and designed to put an extra-smooth finish on your nails. Fisting aficionados swear by these to make absolutely sure there are no rough edges on nails, skin or cuticles.

.17.

Cotton Balls

For those of you who have long fingernails, and for those who simply want an extra margin of safety and comfort, placing a cotton ball at the ends of the glove tips to cover your nails can make a noticeable and welcome difference.

.18.

Diaper Wipes

These can be wonderful for general clean-up afterwards. They contain various cleaning/disinfecting agents along with a skin-smoothing agent such as lanolin. They're also somewhat popular for male masturbation.

19

Improvised Lubes

A typical supermarket or pharmacy will contain a variety of jellies, moisturizing creams, and so forth that just happen to work very well as a lubricant in erotic situations. Some are water-based and some are oil-based. As a general rule, the unscented types are preferred for internal use. Preferences and tastes vary widely in this area, so I advise you to experiment with several different types. ✷ Most improvised lubes are oil-based and thus should not be used in conjunction with latex barriers. They include Albolene (very popular for male masturbation), Vaseline, Lubriderm, Vaseline Intensive Care Lotion, baby oil, hand creams, and Oil of Olay. Over in the food section, we have a wide variety of vegetable oils. ✷ KY Jelly is a little thick and gooey for sexual use, but it is water-based and thus condom-friendly. In an emergency, even egg white – also condom-friendly – can be used.

·····
.20.
·····

Vibrators Etc.

Of course, one can buy a wide variety of "muscle massagers" at various stores. These come in both the traditional penis shape and in a variety of hand-held shapes. One can even purchase a double-headed version. While I'm reluctant to recommend any particular brand, I feel I should point out that the Hitachi Magic Wand, with its tennis-ball-sized head, has been called "The Cadillac of vibrators" by the staff of Good Vibrations. ✳ The hand-held models often come with a variety of attachments, and carefully exploring each can be great fun. One caution: some vibrators come with an infra-red heating element.

While this can be quite useful during regular muscle massage, it is definitely not recommended for use during masturbation. There has been at least one hospitalization for genital burns that occurred during such usage, so be careful. Most brands that offer infra-red come with an on/off switch regarding this feature, but at least one brand I saw *always* has its infra-red in operation, so pay close attention to what brand you buy.

21

Shower Head

This is so well-known that it hardly qualifies as a Trick, but, given that we're covering the basics here, let me point out that the use of a hand-held shower extension nozzle attached to a built-in hose is extremely popular as a female masturbation device. Those that can vary the pressure and pattern of the water and/or deliver it in a "massage" type manner are particularly popular. They also allow a more thorough cleaning between the legs, thus removing residual soap and so forth, than conventional shower heads.

Beyond the Obvious. *Of course, many, many items designed for other uses have inspired Tricksters to heights of erotic creativity. So here goes:*

22

Straw Boss

Grab a soda straw. Blow on an area while it's dry, then wet it (using your conveniently available "wetter") and blow again.

23.

Cold Tongue

Take a medium-sized bite of *crushed* ice, then give him
a blow job. He'll shiver... in ecstasy.

24.

Hershey's Kiss

Fellatio can be made more interesting and
pleasurable for you if you place a small piece of chocolate
in your mouth while you're doing it.
Of course, you may need more than one piece.

25.

Joe Camel

Use a camel-hair art brush on various
tender parts of your partner's body. It
seems to work especially well on the
vulva and inner thighs. This Trick works
well when combined with a blindfold. To spice it up
even more, use a pencil sharpener to sharpen the "eraser
end" to provide alternating sharp/soft sensations.
(Be careful not to break the skin.)

26

Brush 'Em, Brush 'Em, Brush 'Em

An old Trick, dating back to the sixties, is that an electric toothbrush makes a great "undercover" vibrator.

27

Why Knot?

Take a silk scarf and place its midpoint behind his cock and balls. Bring the ends around to above the base of the penis and tie them together in a large knot. Leave each free end at least a foot long. During intercourse, she pulls on the free ends so that the knot rubs against her clit.

• • • • •
28.
• • • • •

Getting Pinned

Ordinary spring-loaded wooden clothespins offer an excellent "getting started in SM" toy. They are cheap, widely available, and relatively "novice proof." For starters, I suggest that you purchase a small bag of them – a dozen or so. Believe me, that will be enough at first.

✳ Try them on yourself first, even if you're more dominant than submissive in your desires. ✳ Apply the clothespins to unlubed skin, using unlubed fingers. You don't want them slipping at the wrong moment. ✳ Keep in mind that, unlike a swat from a hand or paddle, clamps always continue to hurt. Unless you've experienced this yourself, it can be easy to lose track of that. ✳ In addition, it's important to remember that your partner will feel a surge of pain at the moment the clamp comes off. Be prepared for a wince or gasp. It's also considerate to remove the clamp *before* they come, while they're still aroused. ✳ If a clamp is too strong, try pulling its jaws apart a bit to loosen it.

• • • • •
29.
• • • • •

Paging Ms. Pussy!

Want your honey to think about you when you're not around? Place your pager, set to "vibrate," in a strategic location in her panties. Then give her a call, just to let her know you're thinking about her.

30

Man from Glad

Plastic wrap makes excellent bondage material for "mummifying" your lover. Have them stand near the side of the bed and wrap them from collarbones to ankles. (As you wrap their legs, they will become less and less steady, so make sure they don't fall.) Once you've got them nicely wrapped, have them lie face-up on the bed and have fun. (This experience can be made even more interesting by combining it with a blindfold and earplugs.) To get to various "interesting" parts of their body, apply tape over the wrapping and then *very carefully* cut through the plastic wrap with a pair of small scissors.

Caution: your lover's ability to cool themselves by sweating will be reduced, so make sure they don't get overheated. Keep water nearby and give it to them as requested. Finally, make sure you have a pair of paramedic scissors, or something similar, nearby so you can cut them free in a hurry if you need to. There is a definite "learning curve" in plastic wrap play. I suggest that you try a few sessions using only a small amount of it before attempting a really "in depth" plastic wrap scene.

31

Better Than Daiquiris

Ladies, do you get bored in the kitchen?
Place the base of your blender (without the jar) on a low counter or table and turn it onto a low setting.
Press your vulva against it for a pleasant buzz.

.32.
Oily To Bed

Smear your own and your partner's chest, belly and legs with vegetable oil from the kitchen, then have a slippery great time. (Note: you may want to make up the bed with old sheets and/or spread a shower curtain liner under the bedding.)

.33.
Getting Into Leather

If you decide to try spanking games, it's best to start with your bare hand on your partner's bottom. If that seems to go well, then you might try adding other items. A good first addition is a leather glove over your hand. This glove will help cushion your hand somewhat, and add an interesting sensation to the spanking. If the leather glove works out well, then there are many other types of gloves, each with its own unique texture, that can be experimented with.

34

Floss Daily

You can achieve an eye-popping, "sweater-bumping" effect by wrapping the erect part of a female or male nipple firmly but not painfully with dental floss. Use lots of wraps so that the floss doesn't cut into the tender tissue of the nipple. Clothing worn over a nipple wrapped in this fashion provides a constant gentle stimulation that can drive the wearer pleasantly nuts. It's probably not a good idea to try this for more than half an hour or so.

35

Mirror Image

For this Trick, you'll need a comfortable place to lie down (your bed should do nicely), a low level of light, a hand mirror, and a small flashlight. This Trick can be done either alone or with a partner. Use the mirror to look at places on your body that you don't normally get to see. Take your time, relax, and proceed at a distinctly leisurely pace. You can shine the light directly at the place you want to look at (or have your partner do that) or you can make the light reflect off the mirror – or alternate between the two. Take some time here. Look at your genitals, your perineum, and your rectal area. If you're a woman, look at the underside of your breasts. This Trick allows you to see various parts of your body in a manner similar to how a lover will see them.

37.

Tentacle Technique

There is a certain style of plastic soap holder that resembles an octopus lying on its back, with its "tentacles" curled inward to support the soap. The next time you see one of these in a store, keep in mind that a quite knowledgeable lady Trickster advises that it makes a great pad for clitoral stimulation – and it comes in a wide variety of pretty colors.

38.

The Painless Whipping

For those of you who would like to try whipping your partner's back, or having them whip yours, an ordinary pillowcase can work well as an initial, exploratory toy. Such a pillowcase can be used either simply held in the hand at one end or after first being rolled up along its short axis.

39

I Glove You, Darling

Look over at the section that sells cleaning supplies –
especially for use in cleaning dirty dishes.
You may find a glove there whose palm is composed
of a sponge. A knowledgeable Trickster advises
that, when combined with warm, very soapy,
water, this makes a masturbation device of
almost unbelievable intensity. So much so
that, if you're using it on a partner, you
should stay alert for feedback. After all, you
don't want them to suffer *too* much.

40

The Sound of One Hand Clamping

If you find that simple wooden clothespins hold
promise, you can begin to investigate the literally
dozens of other types of clamps on the market.
Plastic clothespins are also cheap and readily available,
and clean up well. A visit to an office-supplies store can
open up a whole new world of possibilities. (One
clamp-loving friend carries dozens of different kinds,
neatly arranged in a fishing tackle box.)

41

This Trick Really Sucks!

The next time that you see a snake-bite kit for sale,
keep in mind that the suction cups can create very
interesting sensations when moistened and applied to the
nipples. After the cups are removed,
the expanded tissue becomes very sensitive to
whatever "follow-up" sensation you care to apply.

42

Scope It Out

Swish some of the "cooler" mouthwash around in your
mouth, then spit out most, but not all, of it.
Then apply your mouth to your partner's
penis or nipple and watch their
reaction. (This might burn too much
to work for cunnilingus, though.)

43

Don't Choke in the Clutch

If you're having some trouble suppressing your gag reflex
during fellatio, try using some sore-throat spray a few
minutes beforehand – perhaps even gargling with it a bit.
The cooling, numbing sensation that results should
help you cope a bit better. Of course, if you insert his
penis very soon after you spray your throat, he'll
receive some of the same "benefits."

44

Gesundheit!

A relatively rare hooker's Trick, and one used only
upon request and with special clients (i.e. those
in robust health), is to take a small amount of
black pepper and wrap part of a handkerchief
around it, thus creating a small ball. Just as the
client reaches orgasm, this ball is placed under
their nose and they inhale several times.
(Be sure to keep the ball well away from their eyes, or
the pepper could burn them!) Anyway, the result is that
the client sneezes several times while they are having their
orgasm. This Trick isn't for everyone, and should
probably be avoided by those who have a history of heart
disease, but those who like it *really* like it.

•••••
45
•••••

When the Lights Go Down
In the City

The amount of light present can add or detract from the erotic intensity of the situation. One Trick, recommended by many, is to replace the regular light switch in your bedroom with a dimmer switch. Doing so can be a bit of a hassle, and even dangerous, if you're unfamiliar with how this is done, so perhaps consulting someone more knowledgeable on electrical matters is a good idea. However, once it's been done, you'll appreciate the results for a long time to come. You can even signal your lover that you're "in the mood" by lowering the light.

•••••
46
•••••

Give Her a Leg Up

Many women like lifting their ankles up in the air during missionary position intercourse. Unfortunately, many find it tiring to keep their ankles up there for very long. One possible remedy is to take a long length of wide, soft material and to tie each end around her ankles, preferably using a knot that doesn't slip such as a bowline. She then loops the midpoint behind (not around!) her neck. This arrangement allows her to keep her legs up with far less fatigue.

47

Squishy & Squashy

More than one lady Trickster has assured me that
the texture and shape of a peeled zucchini are
perfect for masturbatory fun and games.

48

Waxy Build-Up

Dripping hot candle wax on your partner is a
widely known SM Trick. It's best to use only plain
white paraffin candles such as emergency candles
or Hanukkah candles. Remember, the softer the
candle, the more likely it can be used on your
partner. Hard candles tend to melt at a higher
temperature, and their wax can cause severe burns. As
always, try this on yourself before doing it to someone else.

49

Cootchy-Coo!

The erotic possibilities of using a feather are well known.
The possibilities of using an entire feather duster
are still not fully explored. Just be sure to use one
purchased solely for this purpose and keep its feathers
from getting wet or sticky.

50

Men *Often* Make Passes...

While sex is usually about increasing intimacy, one way to add a bit of spice to things is to sometimes make it a bit more impersonal. A highly experienced lady Trickster achieves this by wearing mirrored sunglasses. She particularly likes wearing these while playing domination/ submission games with her lover, but they can work well during more conventional lovemaking, too.

51

Leather 'n' Lace

Bootlaces and shoelaces, particularly if made out of leather, work very well for binding the male genitals. For starters, try winding a few coils behind both the penis and scrotum, then a few more above the scrotum but below the penis.

52

Spread 'Em

Place an ordinary table knife, one that's not too sharp, in the refrigerator, and let it chill for an hour or so. Then apply its blade to your lover's skin. Lightly drag the blade across their more tender spots. The backside of the blade, as well as the flat of the knife, can also be used. This Trick can created the very intense sensation of an erotic "cutting" without producing any actual damage. It can be combined with a blindfold to truly excellent effect, but save that for a time when you and your partner know and trust each other very well. (We don't want to panic them, do we?)

53

You've Got Pull Around Here

Take a nylon or cotton stocking, a narrow silk scarf, a necktie, or any other item that's soft and considerably longer than it is wide, and wrap it around the top of his scrotum a few times, leaving two free ends each at least a foot long. Then have him lie down on his back with his legs open. Sit between his legs and grasp the free ends with your "non-dominant" hand and begin to masturbate him with your "dominant" hand. As you work on him, gradually pull down against his "trapped" testicles. Ease the pressure on up to the point where it's almost painful, then back it down. (No sudden yanking, please. That could harm him.) Keep in mind that he may thrash around quite a bit when he comes, so it may be best to let go of the traction at that point.

54

Chute and Sweet

Here's a Trick that can make anal play a little easy. Put on your glove and slowly enter your partner's anus using a well-lubricated finger – maybe starting with your little finger and working your way up to the wider ones. When you're ready to try inserting two fingers, press your thumb and index finger together and bend them so that your fingernails are pointing inward, away from the walls of the rectum. Arch or curl your other fingers back out of the way. Slowly insert your thumb and forefinger, allowing plenty of time for both the external and internal sphincters to relax.

55

Oooh, Baby, Baby

A mischievous lady Trickster suggests taking a baby's teething ring – "a nice big round one" – and slipping it behind both the penis and testicles to form a cock ring. To spice this one up a bit, you can either warm it up or cool it down before slipping it on.

56

Kindler, Gentler Wax

Many people find the idea of playing with dripping candle wax to be intriguing, but also find the regular candles are too hot for them. (You can get an idea of how hot the melting temperature of any particular candle is by scratching it with your thumbnail: the softer the wax, the lower the melting point.)
One alternative is to use the candles that are sold in tall jars in supermarkets, variety stores, and so forth. Some of these candles come in plain jars, and some come with various religious-type pictures on the sides. The wax in these candles often melts at a considerably lower temperature than that of other candles. Many Tricksters compare it to warm bubble gum.

57

Dental Hygiene

You can definitely make fellatio more interesting for the recipient (as if it weren't interesting enough!) by placing some toothpaste in your mouth before going down on him.
Pepsodent has something of a cult following, as does Close Up.

58

Mirror, Mirror, In My Hand...

You can get an entirely different point of view of things by holding a mirror in your hand while your lover is performing oral sex on you. Hold it off to the side and notice how things look from there. It's almost like watching a porno movie starring the two of you. Just don't drop the mirror! Seven years of bad luck and all that.

59

You'll Pacify 'Em, All Right!

Take a baby's pacifier and put it in the freezer for an hour or so, then remove it and apply it to your lover's "tender bits."

60

Fun With Funnels

Take a small, plastic funnel – a four ounce size is about right – and place the wide end over your lover's nipple, penis, or any other erogenous "sticky-outy" place and suck on the smaller end. (You may need to apply some saliva or other lubricant to the inside of the funnel in order to get a good seal.) Then lift the funnel slightly and blow some of your warm breath onto the skin. Follow this by using massage-like motions to move the funnel around, then repeat the sucking and blowing.

61

Fashion Statement

An undershirt, preferably an old, very soft one,
can make an excellent cloth for wiping yourself off
during and after sex. Placing any long, cylindrical
parts of you inside the neck, sleeves, or bottom
of the shirt works particularly well.

62

Catch 'Em With a Net

A hairnet placed over your hand can make a
wonderful "texture toy." Incorporate it during
various kinds of stroking and caressing you do
to your lover's body.

63

Sock It To Me

Many men like to slip a sock over their
penis while they masturbate. It does a wonderful job of
catching the semen in a non-messy way. Different textures
have their fans, as do different colors!

64

Marinated Eggplant

While several different types of vegetables have their following as female masturbation aids, the Japanese Eggplant, with its ever-so-interesting (and familiar) curve, has its own special, and very loyal, fan club.

65

Cup O' Lube

This Trick can be particular useful as a prelude to anal play. Given that anal play takes an exceptionally large amount of lube, and given that Tricksters don't want to contaminate the jar that many lubes come in, they take a substantial amount of lube and place it in a paper cup, then resupply from there.

66

Grin and Bear It

Don't throw that plastic honey bear away once you've used up all the honey therein. Wash it carefully with soap and very hot water, then recycle it: it makes a great-looking lube dispenser, and its presence on your nightstand is something of a statement.

67

Belling the Cock

If you want to experiment with wearing a cock ring but, for some reason, your local store doesn't carry them, try using a collar for a small cat. It should buckle into place behind the cock and balls quite nicely, and the bell on many cat collars is an especially nice additional touch!

68

One Order of Pasta, To Come

One Trick of special interest is the employment of a pasta server (the plastic kind that looks like a large spoon with vertical "fingers" around its edges) to caress your lover. You can gently caress with the back of the bowl, or deliver spanks with it that range from light to heavy. The tines can be used to stroke various places with the pressure you used again varying from light to heavy. A lady Trickster of considerable experience notes that the eyebrows of her male lovers always raise in a unique way when she uses the bowl to cup one of the testicles.

69
Gag Gift

A fist-sized piece of foam rubber with a strap or rope run through its middle can make an excellent gag. It absorbs sound well, doesn't fatigue the gagged person's jaws as much as harder materials do, and absorbs saliva. *Caution:* A gag consists of two parts – the mouth stuffing and the strap. For safety purposes, the mouth stuffing should be attached to the strap. Fatalities have been reported when the the mouth stuffing has worked its way into the back of the throat and suffocated the victim.

70
Two Cents Plain

A male Trickster confides that "it really works" when he takes some warm seltzer water into his mouth and then goes down on his lady love.

71
Peas Sign

An unopened bag of frozen peas makes an excellent ice pack. Its looseness allows it to be molded nicely to various shapes.

.72.

Roll, Roll, Roll Your Beau

A quite knowledgeable lady Trickster advises me that a
rolling pin can make a wonderful massage tool.
She advises rolling it gently across your partner's back,
then down over their bottom and legs. It can also work
well on the front of your partner's body. Just be careful
around the breasts and other "delicate" structures. The
pressure can be varied according to taste.

.73.

Sock 'N' Roll

She further advises that the surface of the
rolling pin can be covered with a sock that
has had the toe cut out of it. This allows
various textures to be used.

.74.

Rolling Water

Finally, she notes that it's possible to buy a hollow plastic
rolling pin (available from Tupperware, and perhaps
elsewhere) that can be filled with hot or cold water. A
mixture of orange juice and ice cubes, with or
without vodka, is suggested for when a refreshing break
is desired (not to the point of intoxication unless
you're through for the evening, please).

75

An A-Peel-Ing Trick

It has been noted that the inside of a banana peel
slipped over an erect penis in a condom-like manner can
make a very interesting adjunct to masturbation.
It has been further noted that it's better to wait
until a few dark spots appear on the peel.
The less ripe ones don't work as well.

76

A Warmly A-Peel-Ing Trick

To really liven things up, slip the banana peel into the
microwave for ten to fifteen seconds, then (carefully and
slowly!) apply it to the penis under consideration.

77

Feverish Lust

If your partner is willing to experiment with anal play
but is *extremely* nervous about the whole idea,
a wise Trickster recommends starting with an ordinary
rectal thermometer. It's just about the least invasive
item one can use. Of course you should be gentle,
use lube, and don't put it in too far.

78
Gourmet Sex

Try decorating your partner with chocolate and/or butterscotch chips – and for the hard-core chocoholic, with Hershey's kisses. A dab of canned frosting is great for getting them to stick to the skin. The Trickster who contributed this idea notes, "A Hershey's kiss fits nicely in an 'inny' navel, as does a maraschino cherry. The ones with the stems still attached might be nice for this." Of course, part of the fun of this Trick is *removing* the decorations – sex and dessert all in one.

79
Rope 'Em and Ride 'Em

Rope of various types is available for bondage games. Such rope should be relatively smooth to the touch. The most useful thicknesses are between one-quarter and one-half an inch in diameter. The most useful lengths tend to be six-foot and twelve-foot lengths.

80
Butterfingers

If your favorite lube comes in a type of container that is difficult to open or handle with slippery hands, remember that variety stores sell liquid soap dispensers that adapt quite nicely to this "alternative" use.

.81.

Noodling Around

For stimulating the skin, a spaghetti fork works well. The
ends are usually nicely rounded off and it feels
wonderful being rubbed along the skin surface. It feels
nice rubbed along a back, but for real
enjoyment, try the insides of the thighs.

82.

The Key to Success

If you reach the point where you're incorporating
chains and padlocks into your play, one good Trick
is to have all the locks "keyed alike" so that the
same key will open all of them. This is very useful
both for convenience and for safety reasons. Some
hardware stores sell sets of four locks already set up this
way. Alternatively, any locksmith can handle this if you take
the locks to their store.

83

A Rose Is a Rose Is...

Rose petals (or any other floral petals you find
aromatically stimulating) placed *under* the sheet add a
delightful fragrance to the bedroom.

84

You Wash, I'll Dry

All virtuous Tricksters carefully wash their "toys"
after using them. However, the question of where to put
them down while drying can be a bit perplexing. A small
dish drying rack on your bathroom countertop
solves this problem rather neatly.

85

Stand and Deliver

A Trickster of some experience recommends using a music
stand to hold your "one-handed" reading material. Not
only does using such a stand free both hands,
but it also is adjustable to various heights –
from standing to squatting.

86

In For a Penny, In For a Pound

At places that sell massage supplies, it's possible
to buy a device called a pounder.
This consists of a rubber ball on the end of a short
flexible piece of metal and a handle on the end.
It's normally used on the heavier muscles of the
upper back, but its application to the vulva or to the
underside of the penis can be distinctly interesting. Just be
sure to start lightly and build slowly. You don't want the
sensation to become unpleasantly strong.

87

Let the Good Times Role!

Tricksters who enjoy sexual role-playing – teacher and student, hooker and client, horsie and rider, pirate and captive, doctor and patient, whatever appeals to their imaginations – sometimes develop a "wardrobe chest" of props from cosmetics departments, thrift shops, toy stores and costume stores. This may encourage you to break out of your old patterns and try something new, or to experience something new in familiar activities. You can make a game of it, pretending to be different people, perhaps pretending to be on a date, or even meeting for the first time. Let your imagination loose.

88

Take a Quick Belt

Leather belts are time-honored devices used by people who are exploring spanking games. As with other devices used for flagellation, make sure the belt has no hard edges or sharp corners that could cut the recipient's skin. The belt can be used either as a single strap or doubled in half. Avoid using the buckle end, as it can cause more damage than is desirable. Belts are mostly used on the buttocks, although a few people also enjoy having them used on their backs as well. As a rule, narrower belts deliver more "sting" and wider belts deliver more "thud."

.89.

Perspiration Inspiration

Skin that's been enclosed in plastic or rubber turns pink, sweaty, and sensitive. Try wrapping body parts in plastic wrap for a while and then try caressing them, stimulating them with your fingernails, or lightly spanking them.

.90.

Soda, So Good

Also good for massage is a simple can of soda from the fridge or vending machine. If it's too cold for comfort at first, wrap a thin washcloth around the can while rolling it up and down across your partner's skin. It feels delightful, and when you get thirsty, no one has to get up.

.91.

Board but Not Bored

Cutting boards of various types offer a useful means of exploring spanking games. These range from small and lightweight to large and relatively heavy. Their broad surface area helps somewhat to spread out the force of the spank and thus make it less painful and less likely to bruise. Be certain that cutting boards used for spanking games have no sharp edges or corners. We don't want to "really" hurt anyone.

92

Tricks Aren't for Kids

This is kind of a "how to keep custody of your kids" Trick. Kids just should not be permitted access to X-rated items. Explicit videos, sex toys, and so forth are for adults. Various Child Protective Service agencies take a very dim view of adults who are lax about this. Exactly what materials are involved is something of a judgment call. My rule of thumb is that if they couldn't buy it at a regular store, it needs to be kept away from kids. ✳ One solution is to place a keyed lock on your bedroom door and lock it when you leave the kids either alone – assuming that they're old enough for you to do this – or with a baby-sitter who just might like to go "exploring."

93

Lock It Up

As a supplement or a replacement to the above, it's possible to buy sturdy containers, designed to accommodate one or more padlocks, that will fit quite nicely under your bed and secure your "rated X" material in there and away from prying eyes. (Hint: try the automotive section – many such boxes are designed to be used in the back of a pickup truck.)

· · · · · ·
94
· · · · ·

Teach Your Children Well

As a counterbalance to the above two Tricks, let me
point out that it's neither necessary nor beneficial for
kids to live in a "sexually sterilized" home. There are
excellent sex education books that can and should be available
for them to look at. Consult the Bibliography for some
suggestions. Visit your local bookstore and see what's offered.
Some very excellent books have been written
for kids of different ages regarding sexuality.

· · · · · ·
95
· · · · ·

Tumbler in the Hay

A sturdy glass such as a tumbler can feel
wonderful when rubbed across the
skin. This Trick can be made even
more interesting by placing the glass in
the refrigerator for an hour or so before
using it. (It may get a bit too cold if you
place it in the freezer, though, so be careful on that
point. We don't want frostbite here.)

.95.

Eh?

Earplugs can add an interesting dimension to your play. As with shutting off your sense of sight, shutting off (or, at least, turning down) your sense of hearing tends to make your other senses, particularly your sense of touch, seem more acute. ✹ Ear plugs can be used both with or without a blindfold, and both with and without bondage. If you're combining them with a blindfold and/or with bondage, I suggest that you do on only with a partner that you have already played with several times before.

.96.

The Secret Life of Water Mitt-y

Bath mitts are available, some with one side that's smooth and the other that's textured. These are wonderful for slowly stimulating and soothing your partner's skin. Some mitts have a little "pocket" designed for slipping a bar of soap in while showering. Placing a few marbles in that pocket can create a wonderful sensation.

97.

Donna Reed Lives!

A very experienced lady Trickster writes, "I love old-fashioned housewife's aprons. Sometimes it's fun to announce it's time to clean house and take everything off *but* the apron. Feather dusters can be fun in this game, too. My partner has had his nose and toes and other parts dusted quite a few times in the course of house cleaning. Usually stops the clean-up though. Probably explains the condition of our house."

98.

A Spoonful of Medicine

Another fun toy for spanking games, and one very widely recommended, is a sturdy wooden kitchen spoon. These light, very controllable items have a large and loyal cult following.

99

Once More Into the Breeches

A lady who should know advises me that snug-fitting jeans with a button fly (such as Levi's 501s) make excellent dildo harnesses. Simply unbutton most of the buttons, put the dildo in place (you'll need the kind with a flanged base designed for use in a harness), and rebutton the fly to the top, leaving one button undone to accommodate the "dick."

100

Busy as a Bee

Many people advise that beeswax candles have too high a melting point for use in hot wax play. They can cause nasty burns. However, another Trickster advises me that they make a really nice massage tool. In particular, a textured beeswax candle can feel especially good.

101

Chinese Water Torture

Gracious lady, the next time you're feeling a bit bored, adjust your shower head so that it's dripping at a rate of one to two drops per second, then lie down under it so that those drops land on your clit after having fallen several feet.

102

The Washday Miracle

When it comes time to wash your ropes, you can avoid having all those loose coils foul up the workings of the washing machine by first placing them in a lingerie bag.

103

Tired of Crudités?

That various vegetables can be used as dildoes is well-known. One way to make them even more friendly is to put them in the microwave for several seconds before inserting them. Be careful here. Start with only a few seconds and add perhaps five seconds at a time. The difference between the amount of heat it takes to make the vegetable feel really good and the amount of heat it takes to cause a burn can be small, so pay attention and work your way up slowly.

104

The Frosting on the Cake

Your supermarket carries tubes of frosting that are pre-tinted for decorating birthday cakes, and that come with a couple of different tips to make fancy borders or lettering with the frosting. This frosting can also be the basis for edible body-art, and it cleans up easily.

105

Scrambled Soft

Your local variety store may sell a "scrambles inside the egg" device, consisting of a long, thin, white shaft that gets placed into a hole in the top of the egg. You then press a switch and two plastic blades whirl around inside the egg, scrambling it. This same device can be used very nicely on the skin, particularly near but not quite on tender bits such as the nipples. As always, stay alert for feedback, as the touch can range from very subtle to painful.

106

After-Dinner Mint

Many Tricksters enjoy exploring what can be called "menthol Tricks." These involve the application of various menthol-containing compounds, including cough drops, arthritis rubs, and so forth to the recipient's body. The male genitals are the most common place, although some people enjoy having *very small* amounts of them applied in other locations. Menthol Tricks are high-intensity/high-risk Tricks, so please read the entire "Menthol Tricks" section in this book before attempting them.

107

If You've Done It Till You Need Glasses

An old hooker's Trick is to hand the customer a large magnifying glass, then allow him to closely examine parts of her body while she masturbates or fellates him.

108

Capillary Action

One of the first Tricks I ever learned, and one of the most useful, is to place an absorbent towel under the lady's hips before having missionary-position intercourse. Of course, if she's a real "bed flooder" you may need more than one.

109

Reinventing the Wheel

One of the more interesting items used in sensation play is the pattern tracing wheel sold as a sewing tool.
Look for the kind with a zig-zag, not smooth, edge.
You can vary its pressure from very mild to strong.
Just be sure you don't break the skin.

110

Have a Ball

An ordinary rubber ball that has had a small rope or strap run through its middle is a well known and reasonably effective gag. It does pry the jaws a bit further apart than foam rubber does, but nonetheless has a large and devoted following. You can experiment with different sizes to see which works best for you.

111

Licking Over the Traces

A useful variant of the tracing wheel Trick is to run it gently and rapidly across some tender part of your lover's body, followed by your tongue.

112

Keep It Handy

If you don't want to hunt for your vibrator, and feel like making something of a statement to whoever walks into your bedroom, put up a two-pronged tool hook by your bed and hang your wand-style vibrator from it.

113

Keep It Handy #2

If you want to make an even stronger
statement, put up a shower caddy.
Then you can have lots of
things "ready to hand."

114

Pizza My Heart

Rolling a pizza cutter across your lover's
skin can create distinctly interesting sensations. Just don't
press too hard with it. No cutting please. Advisory: If
you're worried about the pizza cutter's
sharpness, roll the edge on some
sandpaper to dull it.

115

You're Aces With Me

Elastic bandages are another type of "homemade"
material popular for bondage games. Because these
can constrict tightly, they are usually applied over
broader areas of the recipient's body, with the legs being
especially popular. They are usually not used to tie hands
together or wound tightly around the recipient's chest. We
don't want to restrict breathing. If the eyes are first covered
with some soft cloth, an elastic bandage can make an excellent
blindfold; again, be careful to not wrap it too tightly.

116

Go By the Book

When you want to keep this book, or any other
kind of sexuality book or magazine, open for reference
while you play, try a lucite cookbook holder – the kind
that holds a cookbook open and protects it
from splatters (!) with a sheet of clear plastic.

117

Totally Tubular

If you find that you and your partner are enjoying
your explorations regarding whippings on the back
and/or buttocks, an experienced Trickster
recommends a bicycle inner tube for further
exploration. He observes that varying the pressure
to which the tube is inflated makes a considerable
difference in the sensation it creates.

118

Romantic Lighting

Is the lighting in your bedroom too harsh or bright?
Try tossing a pretty silk scarf over the lampshade.
(Make sure the scarf isn't too near the bulb or any
other hot parts of the lamp.)

119

Bag of Tricks

Collect a variety of materials with different textures –
hard, soft, smooth, rough, and so on. Caress your lover
with different materials, all over. You can use different
materials on different spots, or different materials on
the same spots. If you are so inclined, the person being
caressed can be blindfolded, so that each touch comes as a
surprise. Some possible materials and ideas:

silk, wool, smooth leather, suede, chamois
smooth wood (perhaps a cutting board)
lots of different plastics with lots of different textures
a rough dishwashing pad
a sponge dipped in warm water
something scratchy (like the pointed ends of
bamboo skewers)
fine-grain sandpaper or emery paper
(try it on your arm)
a hand wrapped in wax paper, plastic
wrap or a shower cap

Use the textures of food items in the same way as above.

120

With Friends Like This...

Tricksters who enjoy anal play often get to the point where they want to clean themselves out beforehand – and others simply enjoy the sensations of an enema. Pre-packaged enema preparations are available over the counter in the drugstore, but many people find them too harsh. Most drugstores, though, carry rubber enema bags (often in the same section as douche preparations). ✳ Enema lovers tend to prefer the douche nozzle (the wider one that has several holes in it) to the enema nozzle (which is narrow and can slip out), but if you're relatively new at anal penetration, you may prefer the enema nozzle. Fill the enema bag with water slightly hotter than you would use in a baby's bottle, but not so hot as to feel like it's burning the skin of your inner arm. Some people like to add a teaspoon of table salt for each quart of water used, which gives the water about the same concentration of salt as is found in your body. Open the valve on the tubing and let a little water spray out into the toilet or sink (this helps ensure that there are no air bubbles, which can cause cramping, caught there), then close it. ✳ Have the recipient lie in one of the following positions: on their left side with their right knee drawn up, flat on their back (a pillow under the head may make them more comfortable), or in the "knee-chest" position, on their knees with their chest and face on the floor. Hang the bag from one to three feet above their hips – use a coat hanger if you need to hang the bag lower than your available attachment points. Lubricate the nozzle very well, and insert it slowly and gently into their rectum. Open the valve a notch or two and see if they can feel the water flowing into them. If they can't, try opening the valve a bit wider or raising the bag a bit higher. ✶ If the water is flowing too fast, they will start feeling uncomfortable; use the valve to stop the water until the feeling subsides. They may need to go to the bathroom right away, which usually means there's fecal matter trapped low in the bowel that needs to be eliminated before the enema can continue. Once they're rid of that, you can pick up where you left off. ✶ *Don't* try for large quantities or long retention times unless you and your partner are both enthusiasts with a lot of experience. One-half quart to two quarts, for five to fifteen minutes, is plenty for most folks. It's a good idea to do your enema one-half hour to one hour before your play session, to give the body time to get rid of all the water. ✶ Enema play is probably not a good idea for Tricksters with a history of colon or heart problems. But for many folks, it is relaxing, sexy, and a perfect prelude to other forms of anal intimacy.

121

Pull Down the Shades

Very good quality, inexpensive blindfolds, marketed as "sleep shades," can be bought at drugstores and variety stores. Take your time and compare various brands. I recommend the type that hook behind the ears and have padding at the bridge of the nose to keep the material itself off the eyes. For safety reasons, I recommend that you not use a blindfold with a partner until you have played with them at least twice. This is particularly true if any sort of bondage is involved.

122

Silky Smooth

If you enjoy keeping those "special" body parts shaved, try lathering them beforehand using a mildly abrasive body sponge such as a loofah or Buf-Puf.

Some of my smoothest acquaintances maintain that this helps obtain a closer shave and prevent ingrown hairs.

123

Plumber's Helpers

Plain metal washers of the kind found in hardware stores can be fun "nipple rings." Roll or stimulate the nipple until it's erect, then draw it through the center hole of the washer.

I suggest you get several different sizes of washers and experiment to find a size that's snug enough to stay on the nipple but not so snug as to be uncomfortable.

This Trick usually works better on women's nipples, but some men with fleshy nipples may enjoy it too.

124

No, No, Not the Hairbrush!

A sturdy wooden hairbrush – again, one with no sharp edges or corners – is another spanking item that comes very highly recommended. Among other things, the contrast provided between the swats given with the back of it and the light strokes given with its bristles can be astonishing. Such a hairbrush was Janet's first SM toy, and remains one of her favorites to this day.

125

Scarf 'n' Sniff

Ladies, try twisting a silk scarf into a loose rope. Hold it between your legs, with one hand in front of you and one in back of you, and slide it back and forth along your pussy to masturbate. Then drape it over his face, or use it as a blindfold or gag: the silk holds your perfume and gives your partner a special olfactory treat.

SUPERMARKET TRICKS

Items to Avoid

This is a book about how to use items that can be found in an average household, or purchased in an average store, to improve one's sex life. However, the following items have a very substantial potential for causing emotional upsets and/or physical damage. Therefore, I recommend against the use of the following items during conventional sex play.

Please avoid using:

* Candles other than plain paraffin candles such as you find for emergency or Hanukkah use. As a rule, the harder the candle, the higher its melting point, and the less suitable its wax is for dripping on people. Colored and scented candles also melt at a higher temperature than plain white candles.

* Clothes irons

* Curling irons

* Heavy-duty kitchen knives, hunting knives, and similar items with an extremely sharp cutting edge or point

* Electric shock devices

* Formal weapons such as firearms, swords, and tear-gas devices

* Fireplace equipment

* Hot rollers

✳ Open flame other than a candle's flame

✳ Sewing needles

✳ Vacuum cleaners

Some of the items listed above, particularly electric shock devices and knives, can be used during SM play by people who have first had expert instruction in their usage. People wanting to use such devices should contact a local SM club to receive adequate instruction prior to attempting to use those items.

Menthol Tricks

This essay has been adapted from my book "Tricks: More than 125 Ways to Make Good Sex Better."

Menthol, when applied to the skin, creates intense sensations. These sensations are usually felt either as heat or as "chilled heat." Menthol-containing products can be used to spice up fellatio (cough drops) or as a male masturbation lubricant (chest rubs and arthritis creams). Their labels will tell you whether or not they contain menthol.

Major Caution: There is a very slight but not completely non-existent possibility of your choking if you perform fellatio while holding a foreign object, such as an ice cube, peppermint candy, or cough drop, in your mouth. Therefore, never attempt such a trick while even slightly intoxicated, and make sure you know how to do the Heimlich maneuver on yourself. (Using the back of a chair helps a lot.) Also, just on the grounds of general preparations for dealing with life, it's always a good idea to make sure that both you and your partner know CPR. Most first aid or CPR classes include teaching and practicing the Heimlich manuever and other methods of helping a choking victim. See "Death During Sex" in the "Help With Problems" chapter.

Please note: Chest rubs and arthritis creams are oil-based, and thus should be avoided in situations that require condoms.

Chest rubs and arthritis creams are used almost exclusively to make male masturbation more intense. They are not designed, intended, or recommended for internal use, so please don't combine them with fellatio, cunnilingus, vaginal intercourse, or anal intercourse. Don't use them to lubricate a vibrator or dildo prior to insertion. I have heard of

●
●
●
●
●
●

some lunatics attempting to use them for those activities, but in most cases such usage was more painful than they could stand. These substances can also upset the natural biological balance of such areas.

A small amount of menthol can, in some cases, be applied to the clitoris to make female masturbation more intense, but please be very careful. Remember, it's not intended for internal use, and it feels much "hotter" on mucous membranes. Ladies, I suggest you try this on your own before involving another person.

Menthol-containing cough drops might be used during cunnilingus, but please note the above warnings carefully.

Menthol must be used cautiously. Whereas other tricks are spices, menthol qualifies as red hot pepper. Using a *very* small amount may spice things up nicely. Too much, and that quantity is very easy to reach, can cause genuine pain, even agony.

Start slowly and with small amounts when using menthol-containing creams. It's often wise to "dilute" it with another lubricant. Never use the extra-strength brand of anything until you've used the regular strength brand successfully several times. Understand that gels can be *much* hotter than creams.

Menthol may take up to five minutes for the effects of a given "dose" to be fully felt, so take your time about adding more. One dose is usually felt for about twenty minutes, but this can vary considerably from person to person and from product to product. Menthol applied to the scrotum is usually felt sooner and feels hotter than menthol applied to the penis.

Caution: It's easy to add more, but it's very difficult to remove what you've already applied.

Another caution: If you use a menthol-containing cream to masturbate a man, a considerable amount will get on your hand as well as his cock. Because the skin of your hand is much thicker than the skin of his penis, it may take considerable time for you to feel this. "Burning

Hands Syndrome" can develop an hour or more after the session. You might therefore wear latex or vinyl gloves when playing with this stuff, particularly the extra-strength brands.

Yet another caution: Be careful about combining menthol with any abrasion. Skin that has been scraped, such as by fingernails, will be considerably less able to tolerate menthol. An amount of menthol that intact skin tolerates well can easily be too much for abraded skin to handle.

If you have a "menthol overdose," you can usually wash it off by using cold running water and lots of soap. Applying large amounts of shampoo and then washing it off works especially well. Very liberal amounts of the astringent called Witch Hazel also wash it off. (Your drugstore carries it.) You can also "cool things down" by rubbing on generous amounts of petroleum jelly or an oil-based cream (be sure you don't use a chest rub!). I haven't personally tested it, but I'm told that cold cream works well.

Don't combine menthol play with bondage until you, your partner, and the substance in question are very well acquainted. A menthol overdose is especially likely to occur the first one or two times you use it with a new partner. If they get overdosed and need to run to the shower, they'll need to be able to run there *now*. They can suffer terribly during the time it would take you to untie them.

It's not a bad idea to deliberately create a menthol overdose in order to test these various cool-down methods. That way, in an actual "emergency," you'll have a clearer idea of what works (and what doesn't). Understand that different people may respond better to different cooling methods.

I don't recommend using menthol with a new partner unless they (and you) are already highly experienced in its use. It's too easy for things to go wrong and perhaps harm your budding relationship. Use this only for self-play or with someone you already know well. It would be a

● ●

very good idea to use a particular lubricant on yourself several times before you ask a partner to use it on you.

Because menthol "burns" for about twenty minutes after being applied (some brands burn longer), and because this feeling may be seriously unpleasant if no longer accompanied by sexual arousal, it's both wise and compassionate to wait for its sensations to fade to a very low level before bringing a man to orgasm.

Final comment: Menthol leaves a distinct and quite notice-able smell in the air. It's a good idea to use it only in well-ventilated areas if the lingering smell might be a problem.

Safety Tips for SM and Erotic Power Play

I consider SM the riskiest form of sex. It has all the risks associated with "vanilla" sexuality, plus its own physical, emotional, and relationship risks.

I have written a comprehensive guidebook to this exciting and risky form of sexuality. It's called "SM 101: A Realistic Introduction" and it's probably available from the same place that you got this book. All of the matters listed below are discussed in far greater depth and detail in that book. If SM is becoming a serious interest of yours, please consult "SM 101" for more information. There is also a great deal of useful information in the "Spanking Tricks" section of "Tricks 2."

I have strong reservations about "quickie" SM instruction. However, many of the Tricks described in this book have something of an SM slant. I'm therefore going to include some basic SM safety precautions in this book. This information is *not* meant to be adequate instruction. Rather, its purpose is to steer you away from the most common hazards.

By all means, check out some of the SM books recommended herein. If you can, contact a local SM club for additional instruction. Also, you can find some first-rate educational material regarding SM on the Internet. Check out the newsgroups alt.sex.bondage, alt.sex.femdom, and alt.sex.spanking, and use the various World Wide Web search engines to discover the many excellent resources available there.

1.   Be careful about who you let tie you up.

Bondage need not be dangerous in and of itself, but it can create dangerous vulnerability. Be aware that when you let someone tie you up, you are literally trusting them with your life.

I strongly recommend that you let someone tie you up only after you have first done at least two SM-type sessions with them that didn't involve any bondage. While all SM encounters have some risk attached, the first few you do with a new partner are by far the most likely to "go wrong."

Subpoint: Limit the bondage the first few times you try it. My rule is that the first time I let someone tie me, I'll only let them tie my hands to each other. I will let them tie my hands behind my back, but I most definitely will not let them tie me to something such as a bed or chair. I won't let them tie my elbows, my knees, or my ankles, or to blindfold or gag me. (Among other things, they're going to need the feedback provided by my voice and facial expressions.)

A common suggestion is "Let's try some bondage. I'll tie your wrists and ankles to the four corners of the bed. It won't hurt." You can see how this is involves far too much vulnerability for a first-time session.

2. Experience it yourself, preferably several times, before you do it to someone else.

The more empathy you have with what the other person is experiencing, the better partner you'll be and the more the both of you will benefit. There's an adage in the SM community that it's better to start out in the "submissive" or "bottom" role. This is true *if* you have access to an experienced, empathetic, ethical partner (lucky you!) and *if* you can assume such a role without too much emotional difficulty. If either is not true, then maybe you're better off not doing that – at least for a while. It is entirely possible and valid to start off in the "dominant" or "top" role.

If doing a "submissive internship" (which can vary widely in its length, intensity, and variety) isn't an option, do your best to experience what they're experiencing. Try applying that stimulus to your own body.

Try kneeling on the floor yourself for a while. Try staying in the position you want them to remain in while bound. (Be careful about tying yourself up – I'll talk more about that later.)

3.   Play with a "silent alarm" in place.

When I play privately with a new partner, I always have what's called a "silent alarm": somebody I trust knows where I am, who I'm with, and what we're doing. If I fail to check in with this person by a certain time and in a certain way, they will know that I'm in serious trouble and things will start to happen – up to and including calling the cops.

(I have called the cops myself when someone I'm "babysitting" has failed to check in.) The primary purpose of a silent alarm is *deterrence*, not arrest of the perpetrator. Therefore, I always let my new partner know ahead of time, as diplomatically as possible, that such a device will be in place while we're playing. Furthermore, I urge them to do the same.

A good partner will understand and not be upset or angry about my using a silent alarm. Furthermore, they will *not* question me regarding details of how the alarm is set up. Any show of negative emotion on their part, or any questioning regarding how my alarm works or why I felt the need for it, are major red flags that I should just simply not play with this person, ever.

If they are new to the practices of SM, I might politely advise them *one time* that such questions are considered out of line. If they continue, it's time for me to forget the whole thing.

4.   Use only plain paraffin candles for hot wax play.

Many people are now aware that it's possible for one person to drip wax from a burning candle onto their lover's skin as a from of erotic play. One major word of advice: use *only* plain white paraffin candles. Colored and scented candles, candles with metallic flakes in them, and candles made of materials such as beeswax may burn at a much higher temperature. People have suffered third-degree burns from having the wrong candles used on them.

Drip a few drops of wax onto your own skin (the inner forearm works well) before dropping it onto your lover's skin.

5. Avoid leather toys that have sharp edges or corners.

When considering purchasing something made out of leather such as a whip, a collar, or a set of cuffs, check its edges and corners. A quality piece of equipment will have these rounded off and smooth to the touch. Shoddy equipment may have amazingly sharp edges and corners. If you find such a piece of equipment, tell the store manager that you're not buying it, and tell them why.

6. Don't whip over kidneys (or liver, or spleen).

While almost any place on the body except the eyes and ears can be struck *very* lightly, heavier blows must be kept away from bone and organs. The head, neck, arms, and lower legs (including the knees) are not suitable targets. In particular, avoid heavy blows to the abdominal cavity. Place your hands on the crests of your hips. Now place them on the bottom of your breastbone at the notch where your ribs come together (the xiphoid process). Stay below the hip crests and above the xiphoid process.

The best area for whipping on the back is the lower half of the upper half. The best area on the buttocks is the lower half. (The inner, lower quadrant is frequently the most erotic place, and is known in SM circles as the "sweet spot.")

7. Clamps hurt most when coming off.

When a clamp is applied, it compresses the tissue and blood is forced from the area. (This means that the area now has no blood supply. Experts differ regarding how long a clamp should be left on, but their opinions are all expressed in terms of minutes, not hours.) When the clamp is removed, blood rushes back into the tissue and re-expands it – and that hurts!

There is nothing that can be done to prevent this pain. (Removing the clamp before orgasm, rather than afterwards, may minimize it somewhat.) It can help to remember that the acute phase will last for only a few seconds (milder residual soreness may last longer), to develop skill in removing them, and to remove one clamp at a time, with your partner signaling when they are ready to have the next clamp removed.

I suggest you experiment with ordinary, inexpensive, spring-type clothespins before buying "formal" clamps. While people can vary widely in how they react to having clamps applied to them, as a rule the more experience you have with applying them to, leaving them on, and removing them from your own body, the better you'll become at using clamps on someone else.

8.   Keep it friendly.

Do SM only with people you know well, and are on good terms with, and when you're in a good mood.

Playing SM with a stranger, with someone you're not on good terms with, or when one of you is tired, upset, intoxicated, or otherwise not at your best, dramatically increases the risk.

9.   Watch out for their tailbone.

A heavy blow to a person's tailbone (coccyx), particularly if they are bent over at the waist, can cause a painful sprain, dislocation, or even fracture. The size, apparent position, and angle of the tailbone varies from person to person. Before giving them a spanking or whipping, take a moment to feel their tailbone. Also, if you move them from a "straightened out" to a "bent over" position, take a moment to feel if it's now more prominent.

10.   Negotiate what you'll do ahead of time.

As I say in "SM 101": "When two people are alone together,

and one of them is naked and tied up, and the other is standing over them with their hands full of torture implements, this is *not* the time to have a serious mismatch of expectations." Adult-to-adult negotiation before playing is standard among SM practitioners. Indeed, many SM folks pride themselves on their non-manipulative negotiation skills. (Negotiation is dealt with at great length in "SM 101." There's even a checklist.)

Negotiation can cover the type and duration of bondage, what sexual acts will and won't occur, what types of spanking or whipping will or won't occur, and many other matters. Experienced SM people can often conduct a full negotiation in five to ten minutes. Less experienced people may take hours. That's fine. It's far better to negotiate more than you need to instead of less than you need to.

Important subpoint: During the SM play, it's important to stick to the limits set by the pre-play negotiation. Going further than previously agreed should not be proposed during the play, particularly by the dominant partner.

11.   Check in with each other afterwards.

The people involved in an SM session need to spend "straight time" (out of role and in a non-sexual context) discussing what happened and their reactions to it. There are three basic check-in times:

(a) Immediately afterwards. No major discussion is usually needed or advisable here, just a brief reassurance that both parties are emotionally and physically OK.

(b) The next day. By now, the participants have had a chance to intellectually and emotionally react to the play. This is the best time to discuss thoughts and feelings, what worked and what didn't, and so forth. This is also usually the soonest you should discuss if and when the two people involved will play again.

(c) About a week later. This is the time to deal with any emotional "aftershocks" that may have come up. It's also a time to deal with any physical problems that may have not been apparent right away. (Both of these occurrences are rare, but they sometimes happen.)

The following SM safety tips are reprinted from my earlier books, "Tricks" and "Tricks 2."

12.   Safewords

To prevent disastrous misunderstandings, lovers need special signals to indicate that one of them *really* needs to have what's going on slowed down or stopped. Safewords fill that need.

Safewords are usually chosen from words not likely to otherwise come up during the session. "Yellow" is often used to signal "let's ease up or slow down." "Red" is often used to signal, "Stop what's going on. I *really* mean it. I'm withdrawing my consent to do this. The session is over."

Failure to honor a safeword is an extremely serious offense – in some cases even a crime. *Never* joke or kid around with safewords.

13.   Bondage Safety Tip #1: Loss of Sensation

There is never any need to tie any body part so tightly that it loses feeling. If some part of your lover's body "goes to sleep," then it's time to loosen whatever's causing that.

14.   Bondage Safety Tip #2: Quick Release

If you tie someone up, you must have some method of releasing them quickly. That means you must be able to get them free within 60 seconds, and preferably within 30 seconds.

One basic safety precaution is to keep a pair of scissors handy so you can cut your lover free in an emergency such as a fire or earthquake. The large, plastic-handled "paramedic scissors" popluar with rescue squads are an excellent choice because, unlike regular bandage scissors, they were designed to cut through leather, webbing, and other heavy materials quickly. These scissors are available at many medical supply stores and at the more health-conscious and responsible leather stores and erotic boutiques.

Both nylon stockings and silk scarves – often the first choice of beginners – are notoriously difficult to untie. Don't use anything you're not willing to cut through if necessary.

15.   Bondage Safety Tip #3: Stay With Them

Many people think it would be fun to "tie them up and then go off and leave them." In fact, this is one of the most dangerous, irresponsible things you can do – sometimes even a crime. If your partner were injured in any way in your absence, even if they asked you to leave them, you could face serious criminal charges.

Here's a simple rule: Always stay as close to a bound person, and check on them as often, as you would an infant left in your care.

16.   Bondage Safety Tip # 4: Emergency Lighting

A bound person needs to be closely watched. In an emergency, they need to be immediately freed. To do both of these, you need light. A power failure during a normal sexual encounter can be annoying. A power failure during a bondage session can be a serious, even life-threatening, problem.

Responsible bondage fans always make sure they have emergency light sources immediately available. Flashlights, especially light-colored ones that are easy to see, are carried in pockets, stored in specific places in "toy bags," and otherwise placed where they can be quickly found in the dark.

Furthermore, increasing numbers of bedrooms and "playrooms" now have "blackout lights" – lights that come on automatically if the power fails – plugged into their wall sockets. Basic models can be bought at drugstores, variety stores, and similar places for ten to twenty dollars.

17.   The dangers of self-bondage

Many people have bondage fantasies but no partner, so they bind themselves, perhaps while they masturbate. Such people face a problem. They want to bind themselves so they can't escape, yet, obviously, eventually they will want release. What to do?

Self-bondage can be extremely dangerous. You know how risky it is to bind someone and then leave them alone. The self-bound person obviously has this problem.

I have heard of several deaths resulting from self-bondage that went wrong. Many of these deaths involved highly experienced players who "knew what they were doing." Most such fatalities involved gags, hoods, ropes around the neck, or other devices that had the potential to restrict breathing; a few involved fire.

Most self-bondage involves locking devices, especially around the wrists. The person works out some mechanism by which the keys again come within their grasp. Unfortunately, failure-proof mechanisms simply do not exist. If the device fails to work (and, eventually, it will fail), the self-bound person often has no other way to get free or summon help.

Also, bondage – even bondage that doesn't feel all that tight when you put it on – can slowly cause numbness. The self-bound person's hands may go numb after an hour. If the keys fall within reach after that – trouble.

In addition to its dangers, self-bondage has other drawbacks. First, if you bind yourself so that you can't get loose, you may rapidly discover that being alone and in bondage is *boring*. Without a "sweet tormentor" for company, this situation can get very stale very fast. The vibrators, clamps, dildoes, and other gear that aroused you when you first put yourself in bondage may feel awful after your arousal fades – even if none of them malfunction or go out of adjustment. If, genius that you are, you set the situation up so you can't get loose for three hours, you may find that the last two hours and fifty minutes last a *very* long time.

Seriously, be extremely careful with self-bondage. It's something that often seems like a good idea in fantasy, and offers plausible exploration, as long as *absolutely nothing* goes wrong. Remember that even a minor maladjustment of a piece of equipment can set the stage for hours of genuine suffering, and that a serious malfunction or unexpected development can cause you to die a slow, agonizing death. You might try binding your breats and genitals, but be very conservative about using anything that would restrict your breathing (gags, hoods, neck ropes), make you vulnerable to a fall (blindfolds), or restrict your limbs – especially your arms.

Many people have died of self-bondage gone wrong. "Experts" who wrote about how to do this went on to die horrifying deaths due to self-bondage accidents.

18.   "One to Ten."

Raise your hand about twelve inches above the receiver's buttocks and let it drop. Tell the receiver that the stroke they just received had a strength of three. A "two" is about half that hard, and a "one" is little more than a light touch. The strength of the spanks can go all the way up to "ten," with each spank above three being about 25 percent stronger than the previous number.

Tell the receiver that when they call out a number, it will indicate both the strength of the spank they are willing to receive *and* that they are willing to receive it. Be sure to tell the receiver that this number can both increase and decrease.

This Trick helps the receiver, particularly a novice, retain their emotional balance. They are thus more likely to open up to and enjoy the experience.

19.   Keep reality out of it.

People often role-play situations (naughty pupil and teacher, disobedient child and babysitter, etc.), to act out SM fantasies. These scenarios often involve someone getting "punished" for some supposed "misconduct." All well and good.

However, it's *very* important to keep "real-world" situations out of SM play. Spanking someone because they forgot to pay the phone bill, left the lights on, or did something similar that you really didn't like, can be a recipe for disaster. These games are consensual, erotic fantasy play, not a place to settle scores or grudges. Those get handled in "straight time," not in the bedroom.

20.   Two squeezes means I'm OK.

An SM scene can create its own intense world for the receiver. Sometimes the giver will want to check on the receiver's well-being without asking a direct verbal question – doing so could spoil the mood. Also, sometimes receivers "go under" into a deep, non-verbal part of themselves.

A very effective alternative is for the giver to take the receiver's hand in theirs and give it two firm and noticeable, but not painful, squeezes. Each squeeze should last about one second and there should be about a one-second pause in between them. This asks the question, "Are you *basically* OK with what's going on here?" The receiver signals back that they are (at least) basically OK with the situation by giving the hand of the giver two squeezes in return. (It is, of course, essential that you and you partner get clear on this point before the scene actually begins.)

If the giver squeezes the receiver's hand and gets no reply, they should wait about ten seconds and then repeat the two squeezes. If another ten seconds brings no "reply squeezes," it's time for some verbal communication.

21.   Avoid breath control and strangulation.

I want to warn you, in very strong terms, to think twice before engaging in any type of play that involves strangling or suffocating either yourself or your partner – a practice generically known as breath control play. There have been many cases of cardiac arrest from as little as one minute of oxygen deprivation and from as little as five seconds of strangulation. Estimates regarding the number of people killed by these practices run as high as one thousand deaths per year, and that's just in the United States.

Some people believe that the "properly applied" chokes taught in judo classes pose no risk of sudden death or other complications. This is just simply contradicted by the facts.

I have discussed this matter with over a dozen sex-positive physicians, and with numerous nurses, paramedics, chiropractors, and other medically knowledgeable people.

None have been able to describe a means of breath control play that avoids the risk of unpredictable, sudden death. As I mentioned, up to a thousand people die from this every year in the United States. Please don't let it be anyone you know.

There is *lots* more to cover, but these basic pointers should help keep you away from the major problem areas. Remember, SM is not just another from of sex play. Its extraordinary risks and its extraordinary potential require that it be approached with knowledge and responsibility.

How to Clean Items After Use

Many of the items in this book are inexpensive or common enough that you can simply discard them after use, or buy several for your different partners.

For more valuable items, it's usually neither necessary nor practical to try to "sterilize" an item that you've used for sex play. But you can remove or kill so many bugs that there aren't enough to transmit a disease. (The saying "it only takes one" is simply not true. It usually takes several million.) In other words, you can reduce their number below what is called an "infectious concentration" and make it difficult or impossible for them to multiply.

Bugs are just like us in many ways. They need water, protection from extremes of heat and cold, something to eat, shielding from toxins, and a means of reproduction. If any of these gets disrupted too badly, soon the bugs won't exist any more.

Imagine your favorite supermarket toy lying over there on the ground with numerous nasty bugs on it. How might you clean it?

First, ask yourself a few questions. They'll determine what approach you take.

Who will this item be used on in the future? If it will only be used on the same person, decontamination isn't as big an issue. (However, if it's going in a rectum, or if she has a yeast or other vaginal infection, it's difficult to ensure adequate cleaning – use a condom on the item to help prevent contamination, then clean it thoroughly.)

If it will be used on others, it will need a much more thorough cleaning. Let's assume it's something you can get wet. First turn on some gently running, fairly warm water. Then put on latex (or other nonporous) gloves, pick up the item, and hold it under the stream of water. Be sure no splashing occurs. The water is physically removing the bugs, so let it run over the item for at least two minutes. Turn the item so that all surfaces are thoroughly washed.

If the item is absorbent, and you know that it's only going to be used on the person it was previously used on, you might stop here. Absorbent toys may retain cleaning agents that can cause irritation later. Place the item on a low-lint cloth, or other place where it won't pick up any foreign bodies, and allow it to dry.

If the item is nonabsorbent, such as a plastic, vinyl, silicone, or metal item, rinse it, scrub it with soap for a few minutes, then rinse it again. (Simply placing the toy in the top rack of the dishwasher can be an excellent way to accomplish the entire cleaning process.) Don't underestimate the value of this step: a thorough washing with soap can remove up to 97% of all bugs. Certain types of soap kill bugs better than others. In particular, nonscented, liquid soaps containing triclosan (such as Dial liquid soap or a generic equivalent) are highly recommended.

Plug-in and battery-operated toys can be wiped with an cloth moistened with bleach solution or alcohol. If you use bleach, a "follow-up" wiping with water or alcohol will be needed to remove bleach residue. Be sure not to get the "innards" wet.

If you believe the item needs a more thorough decontamination, you can soak it in one of several cleaning solutions. Remember this principle: *soak for a minimum of 20 minutes.*

Nonabsorbent items can be washed, then soaked in a solution made from nine parts water to one part 5.25% sodium hypochlorite bleach (common household bleach) for at least 20 minutes. This is a powerful disinfectant with a broad spectrum. *It is the preferred cleaning agent.* Be sure to use a bleach-water solution that's not more than a few hours old. After soaking, rinse with water or alcohol to remove any bleach residue. then set it aside to dry.

Nonabsorbent, and some absorbent, items can be soaked for at least 20 minutes in a solution consisting of at least 60 percent ethanol or isopropyl alcohol. Alcohol evaporates rapidly, so it may be wise to use a covered container. Note that alcohol is not as broad spectrum a decontaminant as bleach and water.

Metal objects can be "soaked" in boiling water for at least 20 minutes. Obviously, other items can't tolerate this degree of exposure to heat.

Leather items such as whips can be very difficult to clean. Wipe them down with soapy water, then wipe them again with alcohol (bleach is more likely to decolorize), and set them aside to dry. They may need to be re-oiled afterwards.

A quiet note about handwashing: more frequent handwashing can do a lot to decrease the spread of infectious disease. (It dramatically reduces the spread of the common cold, for example.) The protective value of washing your hands after you play, and after you clean your toys, is not yet fully appreciated.

Cleaning toys can seem something of a chore at first, but with time it becomes "just another part of it." Also, the time spent cleaning your toys can be a delicious time to contemplate how, when, and on whom they'll next be used.

Oops! - Or, Accidents Happen

What to Do If a Condom Fails

OK, guy, while having vaginal intercourse you look down and you see that the condom you were wearing has broken and you are now wearing a small latex ring around the base of your cock. Or maybe you look down and discover that the condom is gone. (You were thinking that this particular brand caused very little loss of sensation.) Perhaps you have already come. What do you do now?

STOP! Then, first of all, if she doesn't already know, you gotta tell her. Try not to sound too alarmed (she may regard what has happened as a big deal, or she may not), but let her know what happened.

OK, you've told her. Now what? If you're worried about getting a sexually transmitted disease, go into the bathroom and wash your genitals several times with very generous amounts of soap and water, then empty your bladder (and maybe drink fluids so you can "flush out" your urethra some more). One nurse who worked in a VD clinic told me that washing and urinating shortly after sex would reduce a man's chances of getting gonorrhea by 50%. (She had no information about whether doing this reduced his chances of getting other diseases.) Another nurse, who also works in a VD clinic, told me that she spends a lot of her time treating "that unlucky 50%" of the men who had tried doing this and it didn't work.

If you weren't already using a lubricant containing nonoxynol-9, but have some handy, consider applying a liberal amount to your genitals and the surrounding areas. Let it sit there for five to ten minutes before washing it off. Nonoxynol-9 kills the bugs that cause AIDS, herpes, syphilis, gonorrhea, and many other diseases, so giving it a chance to help makes sense to me.

This could be overkill, but after you shower, consider applying rubbing alcohol, hydrogen peroxide, or an antiseptic (Betadine, or a generic version of it, would be a good choice) as a final touch.

What about her? A woman is in a riskier situation. Trying to wash out your semen (and whatever it contains) may drive some of it further up into her body. Therefore, consider immediately inserting two spermicidal suppositories into her vagina. This will place a considerable amount of nonoxynol-9 into her without driving whatever's already in there further in (as the pressure caused by using a syringe full of contraceptive foam might).

Once the suppositories have had a chance to work (15 minutes?), then she can wash herself off, and out. Opinions differ as to whether or not douching is a good idea. While you're waiting, nonoxynol-9 can be applied to her external genital region, and washed off later, to help zap any bugs or sperm lurking there.

Again, this may be overkill, but I'll point out that it's possible to douche with a dilute Betadine-type solution. Also, as with men, rubbing alcohol, hydrogen peroxide, and antiseptic creams can be applied to the external genitals.

If you feel you need immediate advice, call your doctor or a clinic. If it's late at night (when these events tend to happen), consider calling a hospital emergency room. They won't consider such a call out of line.

In the morning, it's crucial (repeat, crucial) that you call your regular doctor, a local VD clinic, or a family planning center for advice. They may want you to come in, either that day or within a day or two, for an examination. Among other things, if you're worried about getting pregnant they can arrange for you to get a "morning after" pill.

Perhaps the most important point of this essay is to point out, once again, that a condom by itself is just not adequate protection. Their failure rate is simply too high and, if you're not using anything else, you may not notice such a failure until it may be too late.

Remember, if you're in a situation where you need to use a condom, then by definition you're in a situation where you need to use more than a condom.

What to Do for a Contaminated Skin Break

In these hazardous times, it's possible for you to get an unwelcome "splash" of potentially infectious semen, blood, urine, fecal matter, or vaginal fluid upon your body. If this occurs on unbroken skin, you're probably not facing much risk – provided you wash it off quickly.

On the other hand, if you get "splashed" on a break in your skin, or in your mouth, or your eye, or on your genital or anal area, you could be facing a very real risk of becoming infected.

It's a myth that "it only takes one" germ or virus or fungus to contract a contagious disease. (If this were true, none of us would live even a week after birth, for we are all contaminated all the time.) In fact, it usually takes several million of the little beasts to give us a disease. Medical folks call this an "infectious concentration."

Therefore, if you do get splashed, the most important thing you can do is clean yourself off *right away*. Don't delay this. Not even for one minute. Take care of it *now!* This is your one major opportunity to reduce the number of bugs entering your body to below infectious concentration levels.

You have two basic tactics: (1) Physical removal of the bugs. (2) Killing as many of them as possible (or possibly rendering them non-infective). Of the two, physical removal usually works best.

For example, let's say some semen splashes onto a bad scratch on one of your hands. Wipe it on your clothing, or a towel, or even on your unbroken skin, as you head for the faucet. Get your hand under briskly running water immediately. Wash it with soap if you have some.

If you have rubbing alcohol, or hydrogen peroxide, or a provodone-iodine solution such as Betadine handy (and you should), employ it at once. Do whatever you can, as quickly as you can, to get as much of that infectious fluid off of you as fast as possible. Among other things, saliva is believed to help render the HIV virus non-infective, so it may be rational to spit on the wound, wipe, and spit again.

If something splashes into your mouth, maybe you can immediately use an alcohol-containing mouthwash, or rinse your mouth out with a strong liquor. Some folks think that rinsing your mouth out with hydrogen peroxide is a good idea. (For goodness sake, don't actually swallow any of these solutions.) If none of these is available, keep in mind that carbonated soft drinks are highly acidic and can kill bugs.

If something splashes into your eye, avoid any of the strong materials mentioned above. Flush your eye with lukewarm water, and plenty of it, repeatedly.

For cleaning the genital/anal area, see the "What to Do if a Condom Fails" section.

Once you have cleaned yourself off as much as you can, there is little else you can do immediately other than perhaps to cover any possibly contaminated skin breaks with a disinfectant liquid or cream. Betadine, or its generic equivalent, would be my first choice.

The next step, and it's *very* important, is to visit a physician within the next 24 hours. (It's probably not essential to go there at once if it's the middle of the night, but definitely go the next day.) Tell them what happened, and what emergency measures you took. They may want to test your blood for the existence of any infection you might already have. Any new infection will take at least a few days, and maybe a few months, to show itself. They may want to take other measures. Each case is different. *Remember:* It's very important to see a physician within 24 hours of the possible exposure.

Finally, let us not forget the importance of preventing such an incident in the first place. While accidental splashes in the mouth or eyes are rare (and we probably don't need to start wearing those face shields that many doctors and dentists wear), we do need to start being more careful about exposing our skin, particularly any breaks in our skin.

Our hands seem most at risk. They're often very near "where the action is" and any break in them can be terribly dangerous. Here are two suggestions.

First, if you're going to play with a possibly infectious person (and such a person can be the very picture of youthful, vibrant health) you might first test the skin around your hands for small breaks. Spreading some rubbing alcohol on your hands is often very effective at revealing breaks.

Second, latex and vinyl gloves are readily available and cheap. I've carried some in my jacket for years, and they've proven useful on a number of occasions. (I change them every six months or so. They get weak with prolonged storage.) Unless you are absolutely sure that your partner is not infected, *wear those gloves*.

Problems

Probably the most important advice I can give you regarding finding help for the problems listed below, and other problems, is to grab your phone book and start looking. Many communities have local resources. Check the first few pages and look over the table of contents. Look up these and related topics in both the white and yellow pages. Check your phone book for an index.

If this doesn't help, go to your local library and look through the phone books of nearby communities, particularly those of nearby big cities.

Local newspapers and magazines, particularly free ones that come out on a weekly or less frequent basis, often carry valuable listings. Gay and lesbian papers can be particularly helpful. Look them over carefully.

The Internet is an excellent source of information regarding sexuality-related problems. Look in the alt.recovery, alt.sex and alt.support hierarchies, in any newsgroups that announce local events and groups in your community, and on the World Wide Web.

Abuse/Battering/Neglect

National Domestic Violence Hotline (800) 799-7233

National Child Abuse Hotline (800) 422-4453

Parents Anonymous (800) 249-5506

AIDS

National AIDS Hotline (800) 342-AIDS

National STD Hotline (800) 227-8922

Birth Control/Abortion

Check your local yellow pages under "Birth Control Information Centers." Note: Some anti-abortion agencies have been accused of being less than totally honest about that fact. If a given resource doesn't explicitly say that it offers abortions, please consider that its policies may be anti-abortion.

Censorship

American Civil Liberties Union
132 West 43rd St.
New York, New York 10036
(212) 705-7496

National Coalition Against Censorship
132 West 43rd. Street
New York, New York 10036
(212) 807-6222

People for the American Way
2000 M. Street N.W., Suite 400
Washington, DC 20036
(202) 467-4999

Death During Sex

People, especially older men, die during sex far more often than is commonly believed. One of the reasons for this is that their partners are often too embarrassed to tell what was going on when the death occurred.

Studies have shown that the person in the community who faces the highest risk of sudden cardiac arrest is a man over the age of 50, and the person most likely to be with him when it happens is his wife. If your boyfriend or husband is over 50, I strongly recommend that you both take a CPR class.

Studies have also shown that the second highest risk group for a sudden cardiopulmonary emergency is, to simplify matters, anyone wearing diapers. If you help take care of young children, schedule a class that teaches infant and child CPR. (The technique differs considerably from that used on adults.)

You can look in the yellow pages under "First Aid Instruction" to find out where classes are offered. The American Red Cross, American Heart Association, some hospitals and emergency service agencies, and private firms all offer classes.

If you take a CPR class, try hard to get a good instructor. I suggest someone who has a minimum of one year of full-time experience in pre-hospital emergency care. A paramedic might be a good first choice. (Although people who are good at providing emergency care are not necessarily good at teaching others how to do that.)

Disabilities

The Lawrence Research Group, which publishes the Xandria Collection catalogs, puts out a specialized catalog of sex toys and advice for people with disabilities. This catalog also contains a page listing of sexuality resources for the disabled across the U.S. To receive this catalog, send $4 and a request for the Special Edition for Disabled People to:

Lawrence Research Group
P.O. Box 319005
San Francisco, CA 94131

Herpes

Herpes Resource Center (HRC)
P.O. Box 13827
Research Triangle Park, North Carolina 27709

These folks offer wonderful information for those coping with any aspect of herpes. Among other things, they sponsor a nationwide network of support groups. If somebody I cared about had herpes, I would make certain that they were fully informed about what these folks offer.

National STD Hotline (800) 227-8922

Incest

Incest Survivors Anonymous
P.O. Box 5613
Long Beach, CA 90805-0613
(310) 428-5599

Survivors of Incest Anonymous
P.O. Box 21817
Baltimore, Maryland 21222
(410) 282-3400

Both of these groups sponsor meetings all over the country. They will also help you start a group in your area if one does not already exist. Incest is one of the most under-reported forms of abuse in this country.

Old Age

Sex Over Forty Newsletter
PHE, Inc.
P.O. Box 1600
Chapel Hill, North Carolina 27515

As people age, their needs and their bodies change. This newsletter is one of the most useful sources of information on the topic.

Rape

As soon as you safely can, call 911, a rape treatment center, or a similar resource. Check your phone book under Rape, Battering, and Sexual Abuse Aid. It's very important from a medical, emotional, and legal point of view to seek help as soon as possible after the assault. Know that an attempted rape can be almost as damaging, and take as long to recover from, as a completed rape.

If you can safely do so, have the authorities come to the scene so they can look for valuable evidence. Try not to shower, douche, brush your teeth, or change clothes until you've been examined.

If you need support or don't feel your case is being handled properly, by all means contact a rape crisis center for more help.

Sex Therapy

You don't necessarily need a formally trained sex therapist to help you cope with sexual problems. Many therapists with broader training do excellent work in this field.

That said, I want to mention that the organizations listed below help train and set policies for sex therapists. Someone representing themselves as a sex therapist would probably have extensive contact with at least one of them.

Sex therapy is not an exact science. In particular, such issues as the use of surrogates are highly controversial. You should understand that the organizations listed below are far from in total agreement on every issue. AASECT is considered the more conservative.

Society for the Scientific Study of Sex (SSSS)
P.O. Box 208
Mount Vernon, Iowa, 52314

American Association of Sex Educators, Counselors, and Therapists (AASECT)
435 Michigan Ave, Suite 1717
Chicago, Illinois 60611

Sex and Love Addiction

These are 12-step groups designed to help people achieve "sexual sobriety" by using the principles of Alcoholics Anonymous. They have chapters in many parts of the country. If one doesn't exist in your area, they will help you start one. (Don't be surprised if your initial outreach efforts draw more people than you expected.)

Sexaholics Anonymous
P.O. Box 300
Simi Valley, CA 93062

Sex and Love Addicts Anonymous
P.O. Box 119
New Town Branch
Boston MA 02258

Suicidal/Homicidal Feelings

Almost every local community has telephone crisis hotlines. Again, check your telephone book – particularly the first few pages.

Additional Resource Information

San Francisco Sex Information, at (415) 989-7374, offers referrals and a sympathetic ear. They most definitely do not, however, offer phone sex.

Alternative Sexuality Resources

As with the "Problems" section, many resources can be found by checking in your phone book and by visiting the library to check the phone books of nearby cities. Also, many alternative sexuality resources advertise in adult papers and other periodicals with an erotic slant.

The internet is also an excellent source of information regarding most forms of alternative sexuality. The majority of sexuality newsgroups fall under the alt.sex hierarchy, but some, typically more oriented toward philosophy, politics and discussion, can also be found in other hierarchies such as soc.*. The World Wide Web also includes a huge number of pages with information, articles, photographs and resource lists on various alternative sexualities.

Important Notice: When writing to any of these organizations, it's wise to include a business-sized, self-addressed, stamped envelope.

Bisexuality

Bisexual Resource Center
P.O. Box 639
Cambridge, MA 02140
(617) 424-9595

Body Size and Weight

National Organization to Advance Fat Acceptance (NAAFA)
P.O. Box 188630
Sacramento, CA 95818

A national support organization, with chapters in many cities, for fat people and their admirers.

Circumcision

NOCIRC (an anti-circumcision organization)
P.O. Box 2512
San Anselmo, CA 94960

Corsetry

For people who enjoy wearing corsets and people who enjoy people who enjoy wearing corsets.

B.R. Creations
P.O. Box 4201
Mountain View, CA 94040
Ask about their "Corset Newsletter."

Cross Dressing

ETVC
P.O. Box 426486
San Francisco, CA 94142

This is a respected educational and social organization for people exploring gender issues and those who care about them. It publishes a newsletter that contains many local resources, national resources, and information on other local groups around the country. Highly recommended.

International Foundation for Gender Education (I.F.G.E.)
P.O. Box 367
Wayland, MA 01778
(617) 894-8340

The organization publishes the "TV/TS Tapestry Journal," a 150+ page magazine containing articles, references and other resources. Sample copy $12. Again, highly recommended.

Expanded Families

PEP

Box 6306

Ocean View, Hawaii 96704-6306

Nationwide organization promoting polyfidelity, group marriage, and expanded families.

Gay and Lesbian Resources

National Gay Yellow Pages ($10.00)

Box 292

Village Station

New York, New York 10014

Again, your local phone book should help you find resources in your area.

Infantilism

Diaper Pail Friends

38 Miller Avenue #127

Mill Valley, CA 94941

This is *not* about adults having sex with children. DPF is an organization for adults who enjoy dressing up and pretending to be babies.

Piercing, Scarification, and Other Body Modification

The following magazines contain wonderful introductory information and referrals for those who are into having more than their nose pierced.

Warning: Piercing, scarification, branding, and other forms of body modification can cause injury or death if done improperly. Proper training and supervision is essential; never attempt these practices without it.

Body Play and Modern Primitives Quarterly

P.O. Box 421668

San Francisco, CA 94142-1668 Sample issue: $12

Piercing Fans International Quarterly (PFIQ)
8720 Santa Monica Blvd.
Los Angeles, CA 90069 Sample issue: $10.00

Pleasure Parties

In-home parties can be a fun, safe and comfortable way to order sex toys, lotions, lingerie and other accessories. Check your local phone book under "Lingerie – Retail" or "Party Planners." A large national provider is:

Coming Attractions Parties, Inc.
200 Valley Drive #10
Brisbane, CA 94005
800-4-PASSION

Prostitute Support Groups

(Mailing addresses only. For sex workers – no would-be customers need write!)

Coyote
2269 Chestnut Street # 452
San Francisco, CA 94123

Coyote – Los Angeles
1626 N. Wilcox Ave. # 580
Hollywood, CA 90028

Prostitutes of New York (PONY)
25 West 45th St., # 1401
New York, New York 10036

Hooking is Real Employment (HIRE)
P.O. Box 89386
Atlanta, GA 39359

Prostitutes Anonymous
11225 Magnolia Blvd. # 181
North Hollywood, CA 91601

For those who want to leave the sex industry or for help afterwards.

Swinging

This form of sexuality used to be called "wife-swapping."

North American Swing Club Association (NASCA)
P.O. Box 7128
Buena Park, CA 90622

Publishes "International Directory of Swing Clubs and Publications."

Sadomasochism

The following organizations are some of the largest. They are open to both men and women. They can provide referrals to those seeking all-male or all-female groups and to those seeking clubs closer to where they live. (Several new clubs form each year.)

Chicagoland Discussion Group
P.O. Box 25009
Chicago, Illinois 60625

Eulenspiegel Society (Believed to be the oldest SM club in the U.S.)
P.O. Box 2783 GCS
New York, New York 10163

Society of Janus
P.O. Box 426794
San Francisco, CA 94142-6794

Threshold
2554 Lincoln Blvd., # 381
Marina Del Rey, CA 90291

Tantra

Tantra, The Magazine
P.O. Box 79
Torreon, New Mexico 87061-9900

Tantra, and its cousins Quodoushka and Healing Tao, are spiritual pathways whose teachings and practices include sexuality. *Tantra, The Magazine* contains excellent listings and descriptions of classes, workshops, and other activities offered around the country.

Transgenderism

For those wishing to change their genders.

FTM (stands for Female-to-Male)
5337 College Ave. # 142
Oakland, CA 94618

San Francisco Gender Information
P.O. Box 423602
San Francisco, CA 94142

Gender Identity Center Newsletter
3715 West 32nd Ave.
Denver, CO 80211

TV/TS Tapestry Journal
Internatonal Foundation for Gender Education (IFGE)
P.O. Box 367
Wayland, MA 01778

Additional Alternative Sexuality Information

San Francisco Sex Information, at (415) 989-7374, offers referrals and a sympathetic ear. They most definitely do not, however, offer phone sex.

Bibliography

"A New View of a Woman's Body" by The Federation of Feminist Women's
Health Centers
published by Feminist Press
8235 Santa Monica Blvd., Suite 201
West Hollywood, CA 90046

"The Complete Guide to Safer Sex"
Institute for Advanced Study of Human Sexuality
1525 Franklin Street
San Francisco, CA 94109

"For Play: 150 Sex Games for Couples"
by Walter Shelburne, Ph.D.
Waterfall Press
5337 College Avenue, #139
Oakland, CA 94618

Condom Educator's Guide, Version Two
by Daniel Bao and Beowulf Thorne
Condom Resource Center
P.O. Box 30564
Oakland, CA 94604
(510) 891-0455

"Sex: A User's Manual"
by The Diagram Group

"Anal Pleasure and Health: A Guide for Men and Women" (Second Edition)
by Jack Morin, Ph.D.
Yes Press
938 Howard Street
San Francisco, CA 94103

"The New Our Bodies, Ourselves: A Book By and For Women"
by The Boston Women's Health Book Collective
A Touchstone Book
 published by Simon and Schuster

"The Good Vibrations Guide to Sex"
by Cathy Winks and Anne Semans
published by Cleis Press

"The Black Book"
edited by Bill Brent
P.O. Box 31155
San Francisco, CA 94131-0155
A comprehensive national guide to sexuality clubs, stores, publications and other resources.

Please Send Me Your Tricks (but read this carefully first)

Do you do something that consistently drives your lovers wild? Would you like to share your Trick with the rest of us? Send it to me! I plan to publish more "Tricks" books. Maybe you can be a contributor.

Send me your Trick, preferably typed on one side of a standard sheet of paper. Please date the paper and include illustrations as necessary. If I use your Trick, I'll send you a free copy of the book it appears in and, if you wish, put your name on the "thank you" list in that book. Because of "independent discovery" it's impossible for me to credit a particular person with a particular Trick. (I repeatedly encountered independent discovery while researching this book.)

Also, again because of independent discovery, I'll undoubtedly receive letters from different people describing the same Trick, and I can only afford to reward the first person who clearly describes the Trick in question. So, again, please date your letter. (Actually, I'll probably send a book to the first three or so people who send in a given Trick.)

You can increase your chances of inclusion by sending more than one Trick. One per page, please. Please don't send more than ten Tricks a year. I wouldn't have time to properly consider them.

Let me know what type of credit you want on the "thank you" list. You may choose between anonymous, first name only, initials only, your nickname, or your full legal name. If you wish, I can also include your city. If you sign your Trick with your full name, be honest about your identity and include your address and phone number. Signing another person's name to a letter is a crime, and I will verify all full names before publishing them.

Please send your Trick only by first class mail. Spare me from certified letters, registered letters, and so forth. If you don't feel you can trust me, please don't send me your Trick. Also, please don't put a copyright notice on it. A unique usage of words can be copyrighted, but not what such words describe. (This is what allows dozens of reporters to each write a story about the same incident.) Also, I'd almost undoubtedly need to rewrite your words while preserving the essence of your Trick.

Please don't send anything too far out or dangerous. Letters dealing with children or animals will be immediately turned over to the police.

Please don't send anything regarding political issues, economic concerns, social problems, and so forth. Again, those matters deserve books of their own. (However, if you know of a widely available resource that can help someone with a personal problem closely related to sexuality, I would love to share that information with my readers.)

I was utterly unprepared for the volume of mail that resulted from the publication of my other books. This will add to my load, and I'm already chronically behind in answering that. I therefore can't promise you an individual reply. Including a self-addressed, stamped envelope will help somewhat, but please don't get your hopes up too far. Also, I won't know until just before publication whether or not your Trick was included, so please don't write and ask. You'll know very shortly after I know.

I apologize if the above seems negative and restrictive, but it reflects learning from experience. If you would be happy with a book and being on the "thank you" list, but wouldn't be too disappointed if your Trick didn't make it, then I would genuinely love to hear from you. This world can use a little more pleasure. I hope you help contribute to that.

Send your Tricks to: Jay Wiseman, c/o Greenery Press, 3739 Balboa Ave. #195, San Francisco, CA 94121.

SUPERMARKET TRICKS

Other Books from Greenery Press

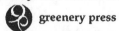